the chase

TH1NK
™

Go Ahead :

TH1NK *: about God*

about life

about others

Faith isn't just an act; it's something you live—something huge and sometimes unimaginable. By getting into the real issues in your life, TH1NK books open opportunities to talk honestly about your faith, your relationship with God and others, as well as all the things life throws at you.

Don't let other people th1nk for you . . .

TH1NK for yourself.

JERRY BRIDGES

the chase

>> **PURSUING HOLINESS** IN YOUR EVERYDAY LIFE

A contemporary adaptation of the navpress classic
The pursuit of Holiness

with Jay and Jen Howver

TH1NK Books
an imprint of NavPress®

NavPress
P.O. Box 35001
Colorado Springs, Colorado 80935

The Navigators is an international Christian organization. Our mission is to reach, disciple, and equip people to know Christ and to make him known through successive generations. We envision multitudes of diverse people in the United States and every other nation who have a passionate love for Christ, live a lifestyle of sharing Christ's love, and multiply spiritual laborers among those without Christ.

NavPress is the publishing ministry of The Navigators. NavPress publications help believers learn biblical truth and apply what they learn to their lives and ministries. Our mission is to stimulate spiritual formation among our readers.

ISBN 1-57683-468-9

Cover design by David Carlson Design
Creative Team: Jay Howver, Jen Howver, Brad Lewis, Eric Stanford, Darla Hightower, Glynese Northam

Some of the anecdotal illustrations in this book are true to life and are included with the permission of the persons involved. All other illustrations are composites of real situations, and any resemblance to people living or dead is coincidental.

Unless otherwise identified, all Scripture quotations in this publication are taken from *The Message: The Bible in Contemporary Language* by Eugene H. Peterson, copyright © 2002, used by permission of NavPress Publishing Group. All rights reserved. Other versions used include: the *HOLY BIBLE: NEW INTERNATIONAL VERSION®* (NIV®), copyright © 1973, 1978, 1984 by International Bible Society, used by permission of Zondervan Publishing House, all rights reserved; the *Holy Bible, New Living Translation* (NLT), copyright © 1996, used by permission of Tyndale House Publishers, Inc., Wheaton, Illinois 60189, all rights reserved; and the *New American Standard Bible* (NASB), © The Lockman Foundation 1960, 1962, 1963, 1968, 1971, 1972, 1973, 1975, 1977.

Bridges, Jerry.
  The chase : pursuing holiness in your everyday life / Jerry Bridges, with Jay and Jen Howver.
    p. cm.
Summary: Explains what holiness is and is not, and shows how we can make it a part of our daily lives.
Includes bibliographical references.
  ISBN 1-57683-468-9
  1. Holiness. [1. Holiness.] I. Howver, Jay. II. Howver, Jen. III. Title.
BT767.B824 2003
248.4--dc22

                        2003015124

Printed in Canada
1 2 3 4 5 6 7 8 9 10 / 07 06 05 04 03

CONTENTS

PREFACE   7

INTRODUCTION   9

CHAPTER 1—HOLINESS IS FOR YOU   13

CHAPTER 2—THE HOLINESS OF GOD   21

CHAPTER 3—HOLINESS ISN'T AN OPTION   31

CHAPTER 4—THE HOLINESS OF CHRIST   41

CHAPTER 5—A CHANGE OF KINGDOMS   49

CHAPTER 6—THE BATTLE FOR HOLINESS   57

CHAPTER 7—HELP IN THE DAILY BATTLE   65

CHAPTER 8—OBEDIENCE, NOT VICTORY   77

CHAPTER 9—PUTTING SIN TO DEATH   81

CHAPTER 10—TRAINING FOR THE MARATHON   89

CHAPTER 11—HOLINESS IN BODY AND MIND   95

CHAPTER 12—HOLINESS AND OUR WILLS   97

CHAPTER 13—HABITS OF HOLINESS   101

CHAPTER 14—HOLINESS AND FAITH   103

CHAPTER 15—HOLINESS IN AN UNHOLY WORLD   107

CHAPTER 16—THE JOY OF HOLINESS   113

NOTES   117

AUTHORS   119

A CLASSIC BOOK – FOR A NEW GENERATION

Maybe you have never read *The Pursuit of Holiness*. But chances are that your parents or your youth pastor have read it. It's been around for a long time, and it has been changing people's lives for decades. We decided it was time to make it a book that you could pick up and experience your own life-change. This is that book — *The Chase*.

We gave it a new title and a great cover, but we also made sure that the words and the stories really meet you where you are. *The Chase* still has all the same ideas that Jerry put into his book back in the 70s, but now those ideas are expressed in a way that you can understand and relate to.

Get into *The Chase*. Find out what it means to pursue God in your everyday life. Learn how to be more like Jesus — to be more holy. Read it by yourself or in a small group. Let this book help to develop your faith, as *The Pursuit of Holiness* has done for so many people.

INTRODUCTION

Maybe you don't live on a farm. Maybe you've never even been to one. But you should be able to get this analogy:

Farmers work hard without knowing how things will turn out. A farmer plows his field, plants seeds, fertilizes, and gets rid of weeds that can kill healthy crops—but in the end he completely depends on forces outside himself. He knows he can't cause the seed to start growing. He can't make it rain. He can't force the sun to shine at just the right times for growing and harvesting the crop. To be a successful farmer and businessman, he totally depends on God for all these things to take place.

Yet if the farmer doesn't do everything he needs to do—plow, plant, fertilize, and cultivate—he can't expect a harvest at the end of the season. He's in sort of a partnership with God. The farmer has a chance of benefiting only when he has fulfilled his own responsibilities.

Farming is a joint venture between God and the farmer. The farmer can't do what God must do, and God won't do what the farmer is responsible for.

Chasing after holiness is like that. Holiness is something we need God to do, yet on the flip side we need to do some of the work ourselves. If God isn't present, true holiness can't be present. Yet if we rely solely on God and don't put any effort into it ourselves, holiness isn't possible either.

God has marked out the path for us to run down, but he's given us the responsibility of the chase. We have to do the running ourselves.

What exactly is holiness anyway? One of the basic definitions of *holy* is "set apart for a religious purpose." Basically, we're called to be like God. Instead of living a life for our own wants and needs, God calls us to be like him.

As Christians, we talk about how we're forgiven. Maybe you've even heard the phrase that says Christians have "power over sin." Even though it doesn't always feel like we have power over sin, the Bible says that the Holy Spirit gives us power to overcome sin we encounter all the time. Sometimes, though, we see this as a "silver bullet" solution. It's easy to think we don't have to change anything to defeat the sin in our lives. We think we can go on living our lives as we please, asking God to forgive our sins, and God will take care of everything. We almost see our salvation as a ticket to heaven instead of a new and better way of living. There are two main reasons for this kind of thinking.

First, we don't want to accept responsibility for our sins. It's easier to leave that to God. Often we pray for victory when instead we should be acting in obedience. We might say that we "fall into sin"—like it's some big hole that opens up in front of us and we can't do anything to prevent ourselves from falling in. Get real! Sometimes sin feels good and we want to do it. But we have a responsibility to live in the knowledge that God has called us to a new way of life. And we have a responsibility to live out that life.

The second reason is that we don't understand what we're supposed to do and what God will do for us. A thought that runs through Scripture says, "We need Christ for holiness. Everything that we bring to God is rags." But another thought, one from God, is just as prevalent: "If you love me, you'll obey what I command." So we have to ask which thought we need to listen to. After you read this book, I think you'll agree that we have to seek out what God is truly saying. As we come to see what the Bible teaches and then face up to our responsibility, will we see any progress in the chase after holiness?

The title for this book comes from the thought in Hebrews 12.

> *Take a new grip with your tired hands and stand firm on your shaky legs. Mark out a straight path for your feet. Then those who follow you, though they are weak and lame, will not stumble and fall but will become strong.*
>
> *Try to live in peace with everyone, and seek to live a clean and holy life, for those who are not holy will not see the Lord.*
> (12:12-14, NLT)

What do you see when you look at these verses? There are two things. The first is action. The writer of Hebrews was telling us to get up and run. Chase after the prize. Our responsibility is to be active as we pursue what God calls us to. The second is what we get out of this—the goal. Do you see it there? It's what we all long for: *a glimpse of God!* If we take God at his word and chase after the things that he wants us to be about, we get to see God.

Remember that the chase is a long-distance race. Don't think you'll get to the finish line in this life and become perfect. That's impossible. What we're called to is a life of holiness. This means that we'll constantly be changing, growing, and learning how to live a holy life. Like a runner trains to get stronger, you'll get stronger even while you chase after holiness. It's a process.

If I tried to tell you that I'd arrived when it comes to living a perfectly holy life, I'd be lying to you. What I know for sure is that God has clearly laid out in Scripture this concept of chasing after holiness. I hope you'll look at this as a journey we're on together. This book is really a travelogue of thoughts and ideas I've put down on paper to help others on the journey. I hope you'll find it helpful as you run along your path.

To get the most out of exploring holiness, I encourage you to go through this book with some friends, if possible. The writer of Proverbs said, "You use steel to sharpen steel, and one friend sharpens another" (Proverbs 27:17). Look back at the verses from Hebrews 12. That writer also said we're supposed to help each other out. If you really want to live a holy life, talk openly with your friends about what messes you up and what you do well with.

CHAPTER ONE

HOLINESS IS FOR YOU

*Sin can't tell you how to live. After all, you're not living under
that old tyranny any longer. You're living in the freedom of
God.* —ROMANS 6:14

Have you ever been to a retreat and come home filled with all kinds of
new ideas about how to live out your Chrisian life? You remember the
last night of worship and how close you felt to God. In your mind, you
know that you can study the Bible and that you're supposed to love
other people (just like Jesus loved them). It's easy, you tell yourself.
You'll go back to the real world and just do it. No problem!

Then reality hits. Monday morning comes and you wake up. It was
so easy last week at the retreat. But as the alarm blares in your ears,
being loving is the last thing you want to think about. Mindlessly, you
eat breakfast and walk out the door, twist the key in the ignition, and
just like the car, your day is started.

*What in the world is that guy doing? He just cut me off! I'll show him; I'm
gonna ride his bumper to let him know I don't like what he did. Oh, wait, what was
it the speaker said at the retreat? That other driver was created by God, and I need
to be loving. Forget that—he just cut me off! Loving—he doesn't deserve it.*

And so your week goes. The memory of what you learned is tucked
safely away in your mind, but it never seems to reach your heart. Life
threw you a curveball once again, and you were all too quick to swing.
Strike one.

After only a few hours back in reality, you ask the question "Does the Bible actually have answers for real life?" You think, *Isn't it hypocritical to feel one way yet live another—to know I'm supposed to love others, while deep inside I can't stand them?* We all know what a hypocrite looks like, and we've all been one at some point. But we also know that there must be another way— some way to just chase after a holy life all the time and not only at retreats, on Sunday mornings, or when we hang out with our Christian friends.

All too often, though, sin gets the upper hand. Obedience, along with holiness, goes out the window.

The Bible does have answers for us. It promises both hope and help. We can walk in obedience to God's Word and live a life of holiness. In fact, God expects every Christian to live a holy life. But before that totally trips you up, realize that holiness is not only expected; it's the birthright of every Christian. We're born into holiness. We can actually do it. Paul's statement is true: sin can't tell you how to live.

The concept of holiness may seem archaic and impossible. It's hard to even think of someone who lives a holy life. If you decided to make a list of people who are living a holy life, chances are that you'd come up with an extremely short list. We live in a day where sex and profanity are everywhere we look on TV, in magazines, and online. To think that we could live a life set apart for God seems almost ridiculous. We all come up with reasons why it's okay to do certain things. Most of us separate our lives into compartments and live out of those different areas, depending on the people we're with. Some friends think that it's okay to listen to Korn, Slipknot, or Britney Spears; others think that pushing the borders of sexual activity is okay.

Some people think that trying to chase after holiness will result in a "holier than thou" attitude. And sometimes they're right. Yet holiness is an idea found in the Bible. The word "holy," in various forms, occurs more than six hundred times in Scripture. One entire book, Leviticus, is devoted to the subject, and the idea of holiness is woven elsewhere throughout the fabric of Scripture. More important, God specifically commands us to be holy (see Leviticus 11:44). It may seem crazy or impossible to try to live a holy life, but God gives us the ability to do it.

Discussions of exactly how to be holy have suffered from many next-to-impossible concepts. In some circles, holiness means avoiding a series of specific sins. You might have heard your parents tell stories about rules against dancing or going to a movie theater. These sound ridiculous now, but most groups have some set of unspoken rules. For some, holiness means a particular style of dress and certain mannerisms. For others, it means unattainable perfection, which can be discouraging every time you sin. When we follow this rules approach to holiness, we're in danger of becoming like the Pharisees with their self-righteous attitude and trivial do's and don'ts.

All of these ideas, while accurate to some degree, miss the true concept of holiness. Oddly, they also provide excuses for not even trying to live a holy life. But you can't let youself fall into that trap. God expects more of you.

So what is holiness? To be holy is to be morally blameless.[1] It's being separated from sin and set apart for God. We've done a lot of talking about holiness without looking at what the Bible says about it. Check out what Paul said in 1 Thessalonians 4:2-8:

> *You know the guidelines we laid out for you from the Master*
> *Jesus. God wants you to live a pure life.*
> *Keep yourselves from sexual promiscuity.*

*Learn to appreciate and give dignity to your body, not abusing
it, as is so common among those who know nothing of God.
Don't run roughshod over the concerns of your brothers and
sisters. Their concerns are God's concerns, and he will take care
of them. We've warned you about this before. God hasn't
invited us into a disorderly, unkempt life but into something
holy and beautiful—as beautiful on the inside as the outside.
If you disregard this advice, you're not offending your neigh-
bors; you're rejecting God, who is making you a gift of his
Holy Spirit.*

Look at how Peter contrasted obedience with the "old grooves of
evil" in 1 Peter 1:14-16: "Don't lazily slip back into those old grooves
of evil, doing just what you feel like doing. You didn't know any better
then; you do now. As obedient children, let yourselves be pulled into a
way of life shaped by God's life, a life energetic and blazing with holiness. God said, 'I am holy; you be holy.' "

These verses show that living a holy life means living a God-focused
life. It's not about doing what everyone else around you is doing (or not
doing). It's all about living out of what God is calling you to. Paul talked
about sexual promiscuity and a disorderly life. Peter talked about evil.
We need to live a life that focuses on the teachings God gives us through
the Bible as well as through the conviction of the Holy Spirit. Living a
holy life, then, means living a life that's in agreement with, and obedience to, the Bible's moral teachings as well as in contrast to the sinful
ways of the world. As Paul put it in Ephesians 4:20-24:

*That's no life for you. You learned Christ! My assumption is
that you have paid careful attention to him, been well instructed*

*in the truth precisely as we have it in Jesus. Since, then, we do
not have the excuse of ignorance, everything—and I do mean
everything—connected with that old way of life has to go. It's
rotten through and through. Get rid of it! And then take on an
entirely new way of life—a God-fashioned life, a life renewed
from the inside and working itself into your conduct as God
accurately reproduces his character in you.*

So, if holiness is basic to the Christian life, why don't we experience it more from day to day? Why do we feel constantly beaten up in
our struggles with sin? Why do we seem to be more like the world than
like God? While this might sound overly simple, the answers to these
questions can be grouped into three basic areas.

Our first problem is that our attitude toward sin is more self-centered than God-centered. It's easy to worry more about our "victory"
over sin than about the fact that our sins grieve God's heart. We don't
want to face up to the fact that we're sinners. After all, we live in a suc-
cess-crazed culture—we should be able to handle this ourselves. But
this attitude takes the focus off God and puts it on ourselves. It's not
about God anymore; it's all about us.

We have to start seeing our sin as sinning against God. Listen to
David's words from Psalm 51. Imagine praying this to God:

> *You're the One I've violated, and you've seen
>   it all, seen the full extent of my evil.
> You have all the facts before you;
>   whatever you decide about me is fair.
> I've been out of step with you for a long time,
>   in the wrong since before I was born.*

What you're after is truth from the inside out.
Enter me, then; conceive a new, true life. (51:4-6)

While David knew that his sin involved other people, he also knew that his sin ultimately was against God. Open up your Bible and spend some time praying about that psalm. Ask God for his perspective on sin. Ask him to help change your thoughts about sin.

God wants us to walk in obedience, not victory. Obedience is oriented toward God; victory is oriented toward ourselves. This may seem like a microscopic difference. But most of us have a subtle, self-centered attitude at the root of many of our difficulties with sin. Until we face this attitude and deal with it, we can't consistently walk in holiness.

Of course, I'm not saying, "God doesn't want us to experience victory." But victory comes as a by-product of obedience. As we concentrate on living obedient, holy lives, we'll certainly experience the joy of victory over sin.

Our second problem is that we've misunderstood the idea of "living by faith" (see Galatians 2:20) to mean that we don't have to make any effort at holiness. Sometimes we've even suggested that effort on our part is "of the flesh"—trying to succeed without God's help.

We have a personal responsibility for our walk of holiness. One Sunday my pastor said, "You can put away any habit that controls you if you really want to." I quickly agreed, because he was talking about a specific habit that I didn't struggle with. But then the Holy Spirit put this thought in my heart: "Not so fast! You can put away the sinful habits that *you* deal with, if you accept personal responsibility for them." Once I figured out that I had this responsibility, the chase after holiness was on!

Our third problem is that we don't take some sins seriously. We mentally categorize sins into areas that we think are more or less acceptable. It all depends. What about the MP3s that you swapped online or a report you downloaded from the Internet? And we all tell "little white lies" almost every day. Maybe you think, *If it doesn't hurt anyone else, then it's okay for me to do it.*

But the Bible says it's "the little foxes that ruin the vineyards" (Song of Songs 2:15, NIV). In other words, compromising on the little issues easily leads to greater sins. And who gets to decide that a little white lie isn't a serious sin in God's eyes?

Commenting on some of the more minor dietary laws God gave to the Israelites, Andrew Bonar said,

> *It is not the importance of the thing, but the majesty of the Lawgiver, that is to be the standard of obedience. . . . Some, indeed, might reckon such minute and arbitrary rules as these as trifling. But the principle involved in obedience or disobedience was none other than the same principle which was tried in Eden at the foot of the forbidden tree. It is really this: Is the Lord to be obeyed in all things whatsoever He commands? Is He a holy Lawgiver? Are His creatures bound to give implicit assent to His will?*[2]

Let's ask the big question now: Are you willing to call sin "sin," not because it's big or small, but because God's law forbids it? We can't categorize sin if we're going to live a life of holiness. God won't let us get away with that kind of attitude.

We'll address the following problems in greater detail later. But take a few minutes to think about these issues right now.

- Will you start looking at sin as an offense against God instead of just a personal defeat?
- Will you begin taking personal responsibility for your sin, realizing that as you do, you must depend on the grace of God?
- Will you start obeying God in all areas of life, however insignificant an issue may be?

As we move on, we're going to look at God's holiness. Holiness starts with him and not with us. Only as we see his holiness—his absolute purity and moral hatred of sin—will we be gripped by the awfulness of sin against him. That's the first step in our chase after holiness.

CHAPTER TWO

THE HOLINESS OF GOD

> *As obedient children, let yourselves be pulled into a way of life*
> *shaped by God's life, a life energetic and blazing with holiness.*
> *God said, "I am holy; you be holy."* —1 PETER 1:15-16

God calls every Christian to live a holy life. No one gets out of it. Holiness isn't something just pastors, missionaries, and a few dedicated volunteers chase after. The Christian student and the Christian teacher, the unsung worker at McDonald's who knows Christ and the powerful head of state who professes faith, are all called to be holy. Every Christian of every nation—rich or poor, educated or uneducated, famous or unknown—is called to be holy.

This universal call for Christians to live holy lives is based on the fact that God himself is holy. Because God is holy, he requires that we be holy. Sadly, many Christians have a kind of "cultural holiness." They're like Christian chameleons. You know what a chameleon does. It changes color to blend in with its surroundings. It doesn't make any effort to stand out from what others around it are doing. A lot of Christians do the same thing. Think about some of the people you know. They don't try to be trendsetters when it comes to holiness; they just want to get by. They adapt to the character and behavior pattern of the people around them. As the culture around them is more or less holy, so these individuals are more or less holy.

But God doesn't call us to be like the people around us. He doesn't want a bunch of chameleons. He wants people who follow him. He calls us to be like him. Holiness is nothing less than conformity to the character of God.[1]

When you look at descriptions of God's holiness in Scripture, you see both the majesty of God and the moral perfection of his nature. Holiness is one of God's attributes.[2] That's another way of saying that holiness is an essential part of God's nature. His holiness is completely necessary for his existence. It's as necessary as his wisdom or his ability to know everything. In more human terms, attributes are part of the "air" that God breathes. God knows what's right and what's wrong, and he can only do what's right.

Unlike God, we don't know exactly what's right. Sometimes we agonize over decisions that affect our character. "What's the right thing to do?" we ask. God never faces this predicament. His perfect knowledge makes it impossible for him to question what's right and wrong.

Still, even when we know what's right, we don't always want to do it. It might blow our cover! That chameleon in us would change to a color that doesn't fit who we're hanging around with. It's at that moment that we choose to be holy or to conform to the world. If we do what's right, our friends will see who we really are. The right action may involve standing up for someone who's being picked on, confessing to something we did (like cheating on a test), or apologizing for something even though we don't want to. But again, this is never true with God. He never questions if something is the right thing to do — because it's part of his nature and essence, he just does the right thing. He always does what is just and right without even blinking an eye. It's impossible for him to do otherwise.

We can describe God's holiness as freedom from all evil. In a simple way, it's like knowing if your clothes are clean or not. When your clothes are completely clean, they have no spots or stains. If you think about God's holiness like this, you start to see that God's holiness is the complete absence of evil. John said, "God is light, pure light; there's not a trace of darkness in him" (1 John 1:5). When you see "light" and "darkness" used this way in the Bible, the words take on a moral meaning. John is saying that God is absolutely free from moral evil and that he's the essence of moral purity.

God's holiness also includes his perfect conformity to his own divine character. That sounds impressive, but what does it mean? It means that all of his thoughts and actions are totally consistent with his holy character—the essence of who he is.

Think about your own life. When you became a Christian, certain behaviors or habits probably changed right away. Maybe you didn't swear as much, maybe you quit being so sarcastic, or maybe you ended an inappropriate sexual relationship. Over time, as we mature as Christians, a certain degree of character or values develop. It happens almost naturally, kind of like growing up physically. But we're not always consistent with our character. Maybe we get into a situation where it's easier to lie. Or maybe we forget to study, so we look at a friend's test. Whatever it is, something doesn't match up to our commitment to holiness. When times get tough, holiness goes out the window. Then we're frustrated with ourselves because we know what we should have done. God's never in that kind of situation. Consistency and holiness go hand in hand for God. He doesn't wake up one morning and say, "I really should've been more loving with that person" or "I shouldn't have taken that shortcut when I created the platypus." He's totally consistent. And it's this standard of holiness that God calls us to when he says, "Be holy, because I am holy."

But don't get all bummed out. This shouldn't be a downer. In fact, it's a huge encouragement. If God is perfectly holy, then we can be sure that his actions toward us are always perfect and just. Think about it— have you ever been tempted to question God's actions? Who hasn't asked the question "If there's a God, why does he allow evil?" or even "Why would God treat me like this?" We complain that he's unfair in how he treats us. But this is Satan's lie. It's the same lie he told Eve. He pretty much said, "God's being unfair to you" (see Genesis 3:4-5). But we know that it's impossible for God to be unfair. Because he's holy, all his actions are holy.

Sometimes we have to accept by faith the fact that God is holy, even when difficult circumstances make it seem otherwise. Complaining against God is like denying that he's holy or saying that he's not fair. In the seventeenth century, Stephen Charnock said, "It is less injury to Him to deny His being, than to deny the purity of it; the one makes Him no God, the other a deformed, unlovely, and a detestable God. . . . He that saith God is not holy speaks much worse than he that saith there is no God at all."[3] Take another look at that quote. These are old words, but they still hold true. Do you see what he's saying? If we look at God and deny that he's perfect (perhaps when we're tempted or when trials come), it would be better for us to just say that God doesn't even exist. Because God's holiness is such an essential part of who he is, it would be better for us to deny his existence than to deny that he's perfect.

Think about this in practical terms. Remember the last time God was calling you to do something? Maybe he wanted you to tell some-one that you'd gossiped behind her back, or maybe you felt like you should help someone who was in a different group of friends than you normally hang out with. We all know what happens in situations like these—it usually turns out badly for us. We do the "right thing" but end up taking the heat. We start to wonder if we'd be better off doing our own thing instead of chasing after the holiness of God.

We end up questioning God when we suffer for doing the right thing. See if this discussion between Job and God sounds familiar:

> *Job answered:*
>
> *"I'm speechless, in awe—words fail me.*
> *I should have never opened my mouth!*
> *I've talked too much, way too much.*
> *I'm ready to shut up and listen."*
>
> *GOD addressed Job next from the eye of the storm, and this is what he said:*
>
> *"I have some more questions for you,*
> *and I want straight answers.*
>
> *"Do you presume to tell me what I'm doing wrong?*
> *Are you calling me a sinner so you can be a saint?*
> *Do you have an arm like my arm?*
> *Can you shout in thunder the way I can?*
> *Go ahead, show your stuff.*
> *Let's see what you're made of, what you can do."*
> *(Job 40:3-10)*

In the end, we need to realize that we don't have the same view that God has. God sees things from a much different perspective than we do. We need to trust him with that. When God is calling us to do the right thing and it doesn't turn out the way we hope, we need to realize that we did our best. It may not be best in the eyes of the world or even the eyes of our friends, but it was best in the eyes of God. We are different (holy), because he is different (holy).

One of the ways we can praise God is by acknowledging his holiness in both our words and our actions. According to John's vision of heaven described in Revelation 4, the four living creatures around God's throne never stop saying,

> *Holy, holy, holy*
> *Is God our Master, Sovereign-Strong,*
> *THE WAS, THE IS, THE COMING. (4:8)*

The seraphim in Isaiah's vision of God's glory also uttered this threefold ascription of God's holiness (Isaiah 6:3). When Moses was praising God for the deliverance of the Israelites from Pharaoh's army, he also sang of God's holiness:

> *Who compares with you*
> *among gods, O GOD?*
> *Who compares with you in power,*
> *in holy majesty,*
> *In awesome praises,*
> *wonder-working God? (Exodus 15:11)*

Scripture uses a lot of different names for God, but one stands out. According to Stephen Charnock, "holy" is used more often as a way to describe God's name than any other attribute.[4] Holiness is like God's crown. Imagine for a moment that God had all his other qualities, such as infinite power, perfect and complete knowledge, and the quality of being present everywhere, but that he didn't have perfect holiness. That god couldn't be described as the God of the Bible. Holiness is what makes all his other attributes perfect: his power is holy power, his mercy is holy mercy, and his wisdom is holy wisdom. More than any other attribute, his holiness makes him worthy of our praise.

But God wants us to do more than just acknowledge that he's holy. He says to us, "Be holy, because I am holy." He rightfully demands perfect holiness in all his moral creatures. It can't be any other way. He can't just ignore or approve of any evil we commit. He can't for even a moment relax his standard of holiness. If he did, he wouldn't be God. So he has to say, "Be holy in all you do." The prophet Habakkuk declared, "Your eyes are too pure to approve evil, and You can not look on wickedness with favor" (Habakkuk 1:13, NASB). Because God is holy, he can never excuse or overlook any sin we commit, no matter how small it might seem to us.

Sometimes we try to justify some action we know is wrong. But if we really get the significance of God's perfect holiness—both in himself and in his call for us to be holy—we can easily see that we can never justify even the slightest deviation from his perfect will. God doesn't accept the excuse "Well, that's just the way I am" or "I'm still growing in that area of my life."

No, God's holiness doesn't allow for minor flaws or shortcomings in our personal character. As in every other aspect of our faith, we need to continue training ourselves to be more like God. Like the writer of Hebrews said, "Seek to live a clean and holy life, for those who are not holy will not see the Lord" (Hebrews 12:14, NLT).

We also need to realize that because God is holy, he can never tempt us to sin. That's what the apostle James meant when he said,

"Don't let anyone under pressure to give in to evil say, 'God is trying to trip me up.' God is impervious to evil, and puts evil in no one's way" (James 1:13). Yet maybe we feel that God has put us in a situation where we don't have a choice.

King Saul felt that way in his first major campaign against the Philistines (see 1 Samuel 13). Before going into battle, Saul was supposed to wait seven days for the prophet Samuel to come and make an offering and ask the favor of the Lord. Saul waited the seven days for Samuel. But when Samuel didn't come, Saul took it on himself to offer the burnt offering. He didn't think he had an alternative. The people were afraid and began to scatter. The Philistines were getting ready to fight. Samuel was late. Saul had to do something! He felt that God had put him in a place where he had no choice but to disobey God's explicit instructions.

But what happened? Because Saul disobeyed God's clear will, he lost his kingdom (see1 Samuel 13:13-14).

What about you? Do you sometimes feel that you don't have any choice but to alter the truth a little or commit a slightly dishonest act? When you think this way, in effect you're saying that God is tempting you to sin—that he's putting you in a position where you don't have a choice.

This may hit a little too close to home, but we have to go there. What do you do with downloading music off the Internet without paying for it? Many consider this no big deal. But what does it mean if you're trying to live out a holy life? Is it okay to steal this music? It doesn't hurt anyone, right? Actually, you're hurting the artists who aren't getting paid—although you may think they make too much anyway! You're also hurting your own conscience (see 1 Timothy 4:2). In God's eyes, this behavior goes against a holy lifestyle. Remember, he calls us to be different because he's different.

Because God is holy, he hates sin. *Hate* is a strong word, but it's truly how God feels about sin. Speaking of some of Israel's sins, God simply said, "I hate all that stuff" (Zechariah 8:17). Hatred is a legitimate emotion when it comes to sin. In fact, the more we grow in holiness, the more we'll hate sin too. A psalmist said, "With your instruction, I understand life; that's why I hate false propaganda" (Psalm 119:104). If that's true of a man, think about God. Being infinitely holy, God has an infinite hatred of sin.

You've probably heard the expression "God hates the sin but loves the sinner." This is true, but usually we rush over the first half of this statement to get to the second. We can't escape the fact that God hates our sins. We may excuse them, but God hates them.

Think about it this way: Any time we sin, we're doing something God hates. He hates it when we cheat on a test, when we act pridefully, and when we're jealous—oh, and when we rationalize stealing music off the Internet. We need to be gripped by the fact that God hates all these things. Instead, we let ourselves get caught up in sin and we don't think twice about it. We have to wake up and realize that God hates it—every time, in whatever way, God hates sin. We have to come to the same conclusion that God does. If we're truly chasing after holiness, we need to see it as God sees it. Sin isn't just distressing or defeating to ourselves; it's displeasing to God. Joseph got it right: "How could I violate his trust and sin against God?" (Genesis 39:9).

God consistently hates sin wherever he finds it. He doesn't hate sin in one person and overlook it in another. He judges each person's works impartially (see 1 Peter 1:17). David was a man after God's own heart (see Acts 13:22), yet when he sinned against Uriah, he faced severe consequences: "Because you treated God with such contempt and took Uriah the Hittite's wife as your wife, killing and murder will continually plague your family" (2 Samuel 12:10). Moses, for one act of unbelief, died in view of the Promised Land without entering it, despite many years of faithful service (see Deuteronomy 34:4). Jonah's disobedience caused him to be cast into a horrible prison—the stomach of a giant fish—for three days and nights just so he'd learn that he couldn't run from God (see Jonah 1:17).

Maybe you're like a lot of Christians—we think we can play with sin and then confess later and ask forgiveness. You've got to snap out of that. You're treading on thin ice. God's judgment is without partiality. He never overlooks our sin. He never decides not to bother because the sin is only a small one. God hates sin intensely whenever and wherever he finds it.

God's holiness and his expectation for us to be holy are good things to consider when you're battling sin. If you think about sin from God's perspective, it seems less appealing. Peter wrote, "You call out to God for help and he helps—he's a good Father that way. But don't forget, he's also a responsible Father, and won't let you get by with sloppy living" (1 Peter 1:17). Granted, God's love to us, demonstrated through Jesus Christ, should be our primary motivation for holiness. But being motivated to chase after holiness because of God's hatred of sin and his judgment on it isn't any less biblical.

The holiness of God is a high standard—in fact, it's a perfect standard. But it's still one that he holds us to. Remember, because he is perfectly holy, he can't do less. Yes, he accepts us solely through what Christ has done for us. Yet God's standard for our character, attitudes, affections, and actions is "Be holy, because I am holy." We have to start taking God at his word if we really want to grow in holiness.

CHAPTER THREE

HOLINESS ISN'T AN OPTION

Make every effort to live in peace with all men and to be holy;
without holiness no one will see the Lord. —HEBREWS 12:14, NIV

"Without holiness no one will see the Lord." That isn't really true, is it?
What was the writer of Hebrews trying to say? At the end of the day,
does our ability to "see the Lord" (which means our salvation) depend
on how we live out a holy life in our day-to-day existence?

The Bible makes two things clear. First, no one—not even the
"best" Christians—come close to measuring up. "We're all sin-infected,
sin-contaminated. Our best efforts are grease-stained rags" (Isaiah
64:6). Everything we are and everything we touch becomes contami-
nated by our sin. As one writer several centuries ago put it, "Even our
tears of repentance need to be washed in the blood of the Lamb." In
other words, even our most noble attempts at purity fall way short of
holiness.

Second, the Bible says many times that Christ is all we need.

> *Here it is in a nutshell: Just as one person did it wrong and got*
> *us in all this trouble with sin and death, another person did it*
> *right and got us out of it. But more than just getting us out of*
> *trouble, he got us into life! One man said no to God and put*
> *many people in the wrong; one man said yes to God and put*
> *many in the right. (Romans 5:18-19)*

> *That's what Christ did definitively: suffered because of others'*
> *sins, the Righteous One for the unrighteous ones. He went*
> *through it all—was put to death and then made alive—to*
> *bring us to God. (1 Peter 3:18)*

These verses teach two things about Christ's work on our behalf. Bible teachers sometimes refer to these as his *active obedience* and his *passive obedience.* Let's use those terms for convenience as we look at what Christ did for us.

Active obedience is all about Christ's sinless life here on earth. It means that he was perfectly obedient and absolutely holy. If we trust Jesus for our salvation, we can tap into this perfect life and it gets transferred to our "account."

Passive obedience refers to Christ's death on the cross. With this act, he paid the full penalty for our sins. Hebrews 10:5-9 says that Christ came to do the will of the Father, "by which we are made fit for God by the once-for-all sacrifice of Jesus" (10:10). Our holiness before God depends completely on the work of Jesus Christ for us.

Take a moment and reread Hebrews 12:14 at the beginning of this chapter. Do you think it refers to the holiness that Christ gives us? I don't think so. The writer of Hebrews was pointing to something we need to strive for: "to be holy." If you don't make every effort to chase after holiness, you'll never get so much as a glimpse of God.

So the Bible talks of two different types of holiness. The first one we have because of Christ intervening for us before God. The second one is a holiness we're to strive after. It might seem that these two types of holiness are almost opposites of each other. But really they fit together like two pieces of a jigsaw puzzle to provide a complete picture of what holiness is. "For God did not call us to be impure, but to live a holy life" (1 Thessalonians 4:7, NIV).

To the Corinthians, Paul wrote, "To the church of God in Corinth, to those sanctified in Christ Jesus and called to be holy" (1 Corinthians 1:2, NIV). The word "sanctified" here means "made holy." Christ makes us holy in our standing before God and also calls us to be holy in our daily lives.

Hebrews 12:14 encourages us to take personal, practical holiness seriously. The Holy Spirit can help us practice holiness in our everyday lives. You might want to ask yourself, *Do I desire to live a holy life?* If the answer is no, you may want to ask the Holy Spirit to put that desire in your heart.

In the beginning, this desire may be just a little spark. But with a growing awareness on your part, the Holy Spirit can fan this spark into a flame that burns for a life wholly pleasing to God. When you first come into a relationship with Christ, you naturally bring some baggage of your sinful nature with you. At the same time as you enjoy those early days of knowing Christ personally, you have a strong desire to be made holy.

We all long for holiness. Two major things happen when we accept Christ:

1.   He saves us from the ultimate penalty of sin—death.
2.   He breaks sin's dominion in us. It can't control us anymore.

Our salvation means that we can be "holy and blameless in [God's] sight" (Ephesians 1:4, NIV).

What would you say if someone told you that he had a fish that lived outside of water? This fish didn't need any water at all. Well, maybe once in a while it took a drink. But other than that, it didn't need water to survive. You'd say that person was nuts!

The same thing is true with Christians. If you were to say that a Christian can continue to live in sin over and over, you'd be crazy! It goes against God's plan for us as Christians. A writer three centuries ago put it like this: "What a strange kind of salvation do they desire that care not for holiness. . . . They would be saved by Christ and yet be out of Christ in a fleshly state. . . . They would have their sins forgiven, not that they may walk with God in love, in time to come, but that they may practice their enmity against Him without any fear of punishment."[1] That's deep stuff. If you didn't totally catch it, read it again. Christianity isn't just a one-way ticket to heaven. God chose us for something far greater than that!

Listen closely because this can be important and even tricky stuff. Holiness isn't necessary for salvation. That would be works-based salvation—you'd be trying to do something to earn God's favor. We all know we can't do that. Instead, we should look at holiness as a natural by-product of salvation. It's a little like the question of which comes first, the chicken or the egg? Well, salvation comes first, but holiness is tied up in it. Paul said it like this: "Salvation is not a reward for the good things we have done, so none of us can boast about it" (Ephesians 2:9, NLT).

Salvation and holiness go hand in hand. When we first accept Christ, we might not think about holiness right away. But the Holy Spirit begins his work in us and creates in us a desire for holiness. You won't find one without the other.

Paul said, "God's readiness to give and forgive is now public. Salvation's available for everyone! We're being shown how to turn our backs on a godless, indulgent life, and how to take on a God-filled, God-honoring life" (Titus 2:11-12). With his forgiveness, God not only saves us from death but also helps us "turn our backs" on sin. You can't separate these two ideas—turning away from sin and turning toward a life of holiness. They're like best pals: they go everywhere together. If you've experienced salvation by accepting Christ as Savior, you not only know forgiveness of your sins, but you can also experience freedom from sin's control over you.

God's nature, character, and essence demand holiness in our lives. When he calls us to salvation, he calls us to fellowship with himself and his Son, Jesus Christ (see 1 John 1:3). This means that God wants to enjoy your company, and he wants you to enjoy his. But because God is light (see 1 John 1:5), you have to face another huge question: How can you have fellowship with him if you continue to walk in darkness?

The answer to enjoying fellowship with God is a word we've talked about a lot. You got it— *holiness!* Listen to David's question,

> GOD, *who gets invited*
> *to dinner at your place?*
> *How do we get on your guest list?* (Psalm 15:1)

David's question is plain and simple. Who gets invited into God's house? Who can hang out with him? The answer—summarized from the next four verses—is "the one who leads a holy life."

Prayer is a vital part of our fellowship with God. Yet the psalmist said, "If I had been cozy with evil, the Lord would never have listened" (Psalm 66:18). What sin are you cozy with? What's deep inside you that you just don't want to give up? We all have pet sins and we all make excuses—usually lame ones—for our sins. When we're cozy with some sin, we're not chasing after holiness and we can't have complete fellowship with God.

God doesn't require us to be perfect. But he does require that we get serious about holiness. He wants us to grieve over the sin in our lives instead of making excuses for it. And he wants us to earnestly chase after holiness as a way of life.

Sometimes it's easy to think that God is arbitrary. But God didn't just make this stuff up. He has good reasons for wanting us to live holy lives. The Bible says of God, "It's the child he loves that he disciplines; the child he embraces, he also corrects" (Hebrews 12:6). God loves us, and he doesn't do anything to us that isn't for our own good. He disciplines us because he loves us and can't stand to see us mess ourselves up anymore.

So what happens when you consistently do things you know are wrong? The answer is in the verse you just read: God loves you, but he'll discipline you as needed. Like a good parent, he'll correct you at the same time he shows you his love.

David described the discipline of the Lord this way:

> When I kept it all inside,
>> my bones turned to powder,
>> my words became daylong groans.
>
> The pressure never let up;
>> all the juices of my life dried up. (Psalm 32:3-4)

When God seems to be speaking to us about sin in our lives, we need to listen and do something about it. If we don't, his discipline is sure to follow. Remember Peter's words: "Don't forget, he's also a responsible Father, and won't let you get by with sloppy living" (1 Peter 1:17). God is serious about his love for us. Out of his love flows the desire to see us live holy lives. That's why he disciplines us—he wants what's best for us. He doesn't like to see us hurt ourselves.

We also need to live holy lives to be effective servants for God. Paul wrote to Timothy, "Some containers [are] used to serve fine meals, others to take out the garbage. Become the kind of container God can use to present any and every kind of gift to his guests for their blessing" (2 Timothy 2:20-21). Holiness and usefulness are linked in a simple way in this verse. Who wants to be served dinner out of a garbage can?

Remember that you're not alone as you chase after holiness. God gives you the Holy Spirit—the Spirit of holiness—to help you serve him and to give you the power you need to be holy. If you go all out with your sinful nature and persist in unholiness, it grieves the Spirit of God (see Ephesians 4:30). This isn't so much about the run-of-the-mill, day-to-day stupid stuff that most of us do. It's more about a life completely characterized by unholy living.

How can you know for sure that you have a personal relationship with Christ or—as people sometimes say—that you're saved? One word: *holiness*. Over the course of your life, you can look at the fruit of your life. True faith will always show itself by its fruits. "Now we look inside, and what we see is that anyone united with the Messiah gets a fresh start, is created new" (2 Corinthians 5:17).

What evidence do you have that you're truly "in" Christ? Again, the answer is that you're living a holy life. John said, "What we know is that when Christ is openly revealed, we'll see him—and in seeing him, become like him. All of us who look forward to his Coming stay ready, with the glistening purity of Jesus' life as a model for our own" (1 John 3:2-3). Paul said, "God's Spirit touches our spirits and confirms who we really are. We know who he is, and we know who we are: Father and children" (Romans 8:16).

If you don't have a longing to chase after a holy life, you need to ask some serious questions about whether you truly desire to be a Christian.

If that statement concerns you, ask yourself these questions:

- Is there evidence of practical holiness in my everyday life?
- Do I desire and chase after holiness?
- Am I grieved by my sin?
- Am I seeking God's help to become holy?

Yes, this is pretty deep stuff. In fact, it's foundational stuff as it relates to your Christian faith. While people have been talking about this for a long time, it doesn't make it any less important. As you think about the questions above, chew on what James gave as a possible answer:

> *Do I hear you professing to believe in the one and only God, but then observe you complacently sitting back as if you had done something wonderful? That's just great. Demons do that, but what good does it do them? Use your heads! Do you suppose for a minute that you can cut faith and works in two and not end up with a corpse on your hands?* (James 2:19-20)

So, what do you think? The answer seems clear. While chasing after holiness isn't just about saying a prayer asking for forgiveness, it's also not just about doing a lot of good things. You might want to read through the whole book of James—it provides a great perspective on living a holy life.

Let's let Jesus have the last word here:

> *"Knowing the correct password—saying 'Master, Master,' for instance—isn't going to get you anywhere with me. What is required is serious obedience—doing what my Father wills. I can see it now—at the Final Judgment thousands strutting up to me and saying, 'Master, we preached the Message, we bashed the demons, our God-sponsored projects had everyone talking.' And do you know what I am going to say? 'You missed the boat. All you did was use me to make yourselves important. You don't impress me one bit. You're out of here.' "* (Matthew 7:21-23)

CHAPTER FOUR

THE HOLINESS OF CHRIST

God put the wrong on him who never did anything wrong, so
we could be put right with God.   —2 CORINTHIANS 5:21

We started by talking about God's holiness. And then we talked about
how God commands us to be holy. Now let's take a look at Christ's holiness. This is important because when we understand Christ's holiness,
we feel secure with him.

As we consider our own holiness—or maybe our lack of holiness—we begin to feel defeated and broken compared with where we
know we should be. Don't sweat it—this is a good thing. We need to
feel this way, because it will push us into Christ's arms. When we understand how messed up we are, we can get a glimpse of how much Christ
has done for us. He's given us his holiness.

Look at these verses and you'll see that Jesus lived a perfectly holy
life while on earth:

- He was a human being, experiencing "all but the sin"
  (Hebrews 4:15).
- He "never did one thing wrong" (1 Peter 2:22).
- Jesus was "him who never did anything wrong"
  (2 Corinthians 5:21).
- "There is no sin in him, and sin is not part of his program"
  (1 John 3:5).

Prophetically, the Old Testament even talks about Jesus:

- God called Jesus "my righteous one, my servant" (Isaiah 53:11).
- Jesus would "love the right and hate the wrong" (Psalm 45:7).

What's the common thread here? Look again. It's that Jesus didn't sin.

Now look at what Jesus said about himself: "Can any one of you convict me of a single misleading word, a single sinful act?" (John 8:46). Jesus said this to a group of Pharisees—a pretty bold move, since they were the religious leaders of the day and thought they lived devout lives. The Pharisees thought they had it all figured out—until Jesus came. He turned their world upside down. This incident is significant simply because Jesus dared to ask this question of the Pharisees. They hated Jesus. If any group of people was ready to point out Jesus' sin, it was these guys. He called them snakes and children of the devil. What an opening this question gave them! They must have started listing his sins, right? Wrong. No one said a word.

The disciples would have been with Jesus. They traveled all over the region with him. They saw him when he woke up, when he was hungry, and when things weren't going his way. If Jesus had ever spoken a sinful word or committed a sinful act, the disciples would have known about it. But they weren't shocked to hear Jesus ask this question. These guys knew that Jesus was without sin and that the Pharisees couldn't level any truthful accusation against him.

But this still isn't the whole picture. Jesus was totally in tune with what God wanted him to do. He knew from the beginning what he'd left heaven for. He said, "I came . . . not to follow my own whim but to accomplish the will of the One who sent me" (John 6:38). Another time he said, "The food that keeps me going is that I do the will of the One who sent me, finishing the work he started" (John 4:34).

Jesus' holiness didn't include just what he did and thought. It also involved his motives and attitudes. Think about that for a minute: What if God wanted not only to see you change externally — how you treat others, how you react in certain situations? Instead, what if the thing that really pleased him was how your attitudes changed? What if you could honestly say, "I'm nice to people, not only because God tells me to, but because I have a genuine love for them. I now look at them as people who have the imprint of their Creator. I love them because God loves them"?

The reality is that we can totally do the right thing, but God looks deeper than that. He examines what's going on in our hearts. Holiness goes below the skin, to our attitudes and motives. Of course, you shouldn't take that to mean that you shouldn't do something just because your heart's not in it. You'd be saying, "Well, God doesn't like it if I do the right thing when my motivation is wrong, so I may as well go ahead and do the wrong thing. At least that way I'll be true to myself." While the last part of that idea could be true (at least you'd be consistent), God can even use our wrong motivations for good. Sometimes he'll even redeem those negative qualities, and we may see our attitude or motive change.

Well, we weren't going to talk about us here. We're supposed to be talking about Jesus' holiness. Even Jesus' motivations were in tune with what God wanted. He was perfect! And since he was perfect, he was able to do something that no one else could ever do — stand in our place before God and give us freedom when we trust in him (see Galatians 4:4-5).

When you start to think about all this holiness, you'll probably come to the same conclusion the prophet Isaiah came to:

> *Doom! It's Doomsday!*
> > *I'm as good as dead!*
> *Every word I've ever spoken is tainted —*
> > *blasphemous even!*
> *And the people I live with talk the same way,*
> > *using words that corrupt and desecrate.*
> *And here I've looked God in the face!*
> > *The King! GOD-of-the-Angel-Armies! (Isaiah 6:5)*

After we look at ourselves honestly and see how messed up we are, and then we look at how perfect and sinless God is, we can't help but see how far off we truly are. God's perfection and purity serve as a magnifying glass, and everything we've done wrong looks huge under it. All we can see through that lens is our sin. It doesn't feel good. But wait.

Two verses later we see the hope:

> *Look. This coal has touched your lips.*
> > *Gone your guilt,*
> > *your sins wiped out. (Isaiah 6:7)*

We all should memorize this verse. God pours out a huge amount of love in these words. Jesus is like the ultimate coal; he came to touch us and make us clean. You may think that after a while you wouldn't need this touch. But the more you grow in holiness as a Christian, the more you need it. Even as you sin less, the sin that remains becomes almost overwhelming. It's that magnifying-glass effect. So we need the assurance of God's unconditional love for us, through Christ. Paul said it best: "God put the wrong on him who never did anything wrong, so we could be put right with God" (2 Corinthians 5:21).

You've heard it a million times. God loves you and accepts you because of how Jesus lived his life. Jesus was righteous. It sounds simple. So why are we talking about this now? Satan (who is also know as the Accuser) loves to discourage us. If he can get you thinking that you might not truly be a Christian, he can lure you back into sin. But you need to remember that God accepts you, not because of what you've done, but because of what Jesus did for you. Rest in that fact. Read and study about it. But above all, don't forget it! No matter how aware we become of our sin, it shouldn't discourage us and make us run from God. In fact, it should make us run toward God and right into Jesus' open arms! That's when we'll really grow as Christians.

As you begin to think and pray about holiness, God will reveal things to you that he wants to help you change. Don't shrink away from them. Face them head-on and determine to bring them back before God. He knows about them anyway. Ask him for help with your battles—the small skirmishes and the major wars—knowing that he'll give you the strength to win. To help this sink in, concentrate on this promise from Ephesians 1:7-8: "Because of the sacrifice of the Messiah, his blood poured out on the altar of the Cross, we're a free people—free of penalties and punishments chalked up by all our misdeeds. And not just barely free, either. *Abundantly* free!"

As you chase after holiness, you should find yourself running to Jesus. You run to him, not because you need to accept him as Savior again, but because he'll lavish his love on you. Because of his love, in your heart you'll know that you're his child. And not just his child but a child who he died for and gave his righteousness to. You can begin to understand a little deeper what Paul meant when he said, "Here's a word you can take to heart and depend on: Jesus Christ came into the world to save sinners. I'm proof—Public Sinner Number One—of someone who could never have made it apart from sheer mercy" (1 Timothy 1:15-16).

Could there be another reason to look at Christ's holiness? Yes. It's important to examine his holiness because he can be an example for us. He provides a blueprint that we can check out to see what areas of our lives we should change. Peter said it this way:

> *This is the kind of life you've been invited into, the kind of life Christ lived. He suffered everything that came his way so you would know that it could be done, and also know how to do it, step-by-step.*
>   *He never did one thing wrong,*
>   *Not once said anything amiss. (1 Peter 2:21-22)*

Paul said it even more plainly: "Watch what God does, and then you do it, like children who learn proper behavior from their parents" (Ephesians 5:1).

Are you willing to take up this challenge? Would you start to look at all the different areas of your life in a new way? What about that test you cheated on? What about that girl (or guy) you eyed and thought about a little too long? What about those things you said when that other driver cut you off on the highway? What about the time your parents were upset with you and you did what they wanted you to, but your heart wasn't in it? What about . . .? The list is endless.

But what if you started asking yourself, "Will this please God?" Whoa! That's way too close to home—you're probably squirming now! Let's play out this scenario:

There's this guy—it's always a guy, right?—who is a jerk to you all the time. He picks at the smallest things you do and even takes them out of context. He blows things out of proportion and is just an all-around jerk. Your gut-level reaction is to be a jerk back to him. But following on the heels of your reaction, you should ask yourself this question: "What attitudes and thoughts would Jesus have toward this 'jerk'?" Ouch! You know the answer. Jesus would love him. So what do you need to do? Take on the eyes of Jesus and see this person, no longer as a jerk, but as someone Jesus loves and died for. Oh, that's tough.

In the words of nineteenth-century Scottish theologian John Brown, "Holiness does not consist in mystic speculations, enthusiastic fervours, or uncommanded austerities; it consists in thinking as God thinks, and willing as God wills."[1] In other words, holiness isn't something we can magically conjure up. It comes from doing as God would do in the same situation. Jesus said, "I'm here to do it your way, O God, the way it's described in your Book" (Hebrews 10:7). We're supposed to follow that example. In everything we think, in everything we do, and in all that we are, we need to follow Jesus and do what God wants us to do. The path we run down is difficult at times, but if we want to see God, we must follow it as we chase after holiness.

CHAPTER FIVE

A CHANGE OF KINGDOMS

Our old way of life was nailed to the Cross with Christ, a decisive end to that sin-miserable life—no longer at sin's every beck and call! —ROMANS 6:6

As Christians, most of us really do want to please God. On some level, we desire to live a holy life. But let's face it: most of us also believe it's impossible. At times, we seem to have great control over our sin. We can go days or weeks without significantly struggling with our own personal sin issues. But then we get blindsided with the truth about who we are—sinners saved by a sovereign God.

Does it seem like the same issues and sins always come creeping back into your life? These sins might be something that other people wouldn't think twice about doing. But for you, it's sin. Maybe you even give up and decide that it doesn't really matter—you just settle into a pattern and become comfortable with your sins. It's not supposed to be that way! Look at Romans 6:6-7:

Could it be any clearer? Our old way of life was nailed to the Cross with Christ, a decisive end to that sin-miserable life—no longer at sin's every beck and call! What we believe is this: If we get included in Christ's sin-conquering death, we also get included in his life-saving resurrection.

Do you see the answer in there? We don't have to live like sin is controlling us. We can move beyond all that. Unfortunately, for most of us, that freedom passes us by. We end up frustrated.

Why? Part of it is how we go about getting help with our sins. How many times have you heard someone say the following?

- "Just get over it. Don't let it control you anymore!"
- "You just need to pray about that. You must not be praying enough."
- "Here, read this book and it will help you out. It gives you three easy steps to overcoming evil thoughts."

Get real! If the answer were that easy, wouldn't all the world's problems be solved by now? If people could control their sins as easy as one, two, three, that would be great. But can you think of anyone who can do that?

After you have tried all the "three easy steps" solutions and have gotten beaten up when they failed, you might decide that you'll just figure out what God wants you to do and then do it. You know, read the Bible, talk with mature Christians, and then do what's right. But your sins just keep coming back anyway. What you thought was dead and buried (that old self) somehow keeps resurrecting itself and clawing its way back into your life—almost like a bad horror flick with zombies!

At this point, you know you have a problem. You turn back to your Christian friends, and they give you one of those trite, fortune-cookie-sounding sayings:

- "You're living in the flesh." (And you think, *Duh! That's what my body is made of!*)

- "You need to stop trying and start trusting." (*Oh yeah, that's what it is.*)
- "Just let go and let God!" (*I don't know about you, but I'd be more than happy to let go, but it doesn't seem to help much.*)
- "Just turn that sin over to Jesus." (*Didn't I do that when I became a Christian?*)

And of course, if you do any or all of those things, you'll no longer have your little sin issue. Right. Your friends who mean to help you out— they're just wrong.

In the end, you probably struggle with the same old sins (and some new ones, too): pride, jealousy, impatience, hatred, and lust. Maybe you still waste your time, criticize others, lie (even just a little), and take part in other sins, all the time hating yourself for doing them.

Then you start to think: *I must be the only one who can't get this Christian life right. Why can't I do this?* You don't understand that everyone else around you is feeling the same way. It's just an unwritten law that no one talks about their problems. You feel like a big loser because no one clues you in. At this point, all seems lost. Hope disappears. You think that the promises of a wonderful Christian life will never come true for you.

Let's get past all the trite sayings and try to make our lives a little bit more bearable. In Romans 6, God promises to help us out, and he also gives us clear responsibilities. "That means you must not give sin a vote in the way you conduct your lives. Don't give it the time of day" (Romans 6:12). Paul was saying that if you expect to live a holy life, you can't allow sin to control you. This is something we have to do. Holiness doesn't come easy; we have to work at it.

Note that Paul started out the sentence with "That means." He was saying, "I've just told you something important, and it's based on what I just said: 'Don't let sin have any part of your life.'" So, if we're supposed to chase after holiness because of "something important," just what is that important something?

In the first two verses of Romans 6, Paul asked, "So what do we do? Keep on sinning so God can keep on forgiving?" Then he answers himself, "I should hope not! If we've left the country where sin is sovereign, how can we still live in our old house there?" Paul was saying that we "died to sin"—we packed our bags and left the country where sin is sovereign. We shouldn't let sin control our lives anymore.

That's easy enough to imagine, but what exactly did Paul mean? What does it look like in real life, Paul? It means that as the result of our relationship with Christ, we died to sin. Because he died to sin, we died to sin. It's clear here that dying to sin isn't something we do but something Christ has done.

When we accept Christ, dying to sin is a fact. We can't make it more or less true; it's just the way it is. Since Christ died to sin, everyone who trusts in him also dies to sin. We can't make this happen. We can't speak it into existence. It just is.

But how this works can be easy to misunderstand. We might think that because we've died to sin, it can't touch us. However, just acknowledging it doesn't keep our sin away. We have to take action. We must use our will and not let sin control us.

Let's break this down further. What does the expression "died to sin" mean? Simply put, it means that sin has no control over us. What did life look like before we "died to sin"? We lived in that other country—the country ruled by sin and Satan. Check out these verses:

- We "let the world, which doesn't know the first thing about living, tell [us] how to live" (Ephesians 2:2).
- We were under the power of Satan (see Acts 26:18).
- We were under the control of darkness (see Colossians 1:13).
- We were slaves of sin (see Romans 6:17).

Everyone who has ever been born, except for Jesus, has been born into and under the power of sin and Satan.

Jesus changes all that. When we enter into a relationship with Christ, we have died to all of that sin. Check out what the Bible says about that:

- We've been set free from sin (see Romans 6:18).
- We're rescued from the dominion of darkness (see Colossians 1:13).
- We've been turned from the power of Satan to God (see Acts 26:18).

Now we're free from the power of sin. We've moved out of that country. We're in the country of freedom and life. We're in God's kingdom now![1]

We didn't really know any better before Christ. When you grow up in a family, you learn that certain behaviors and actions are normal. It's like that growing up in the family of sinners, too. As humans, we sin because it's just what we do. The Bible says that we were slaves to sin, although we didn't know it. It doesn't matter that we did some good things—at our core we were sinners! And we know how God feels about sin.

Jesus comes and saves us from this land of sin. So why do we cross the border and go back to that country? We won't be fully cleansed from sin until we stand before God. Our sin nature still lives in us, and it wants out. It wants to see evil come to life. Remember those horror movie zombies—they keep coming out.

An illustration from war shows how this is true. It's civil war, with two competing parties fighting for control. Eventually, with the help of an outside army, one side wins the war and assumes control of the nation's government. But the losing side doesn't stop fighting—they simply change their tactics to guerrilla warfare and continue to fight. In fact, the "losing" side is so successful that the country supplying outside help can't withdraw its troops.

It's like that with us. Satan's been kicked in the teeth and he's already lost the war. But even though he's lost, he resorts to guerrilla warfare. Through our sinful nature, he leads us back into sin. This is where the big struggle happens.

> *There is a root of sinful self-interest in us that is at odds with a free spirit, just as the free spirit is incompatible with selfishness. These two ways of life are antithetical, so that you cannot live at times one way and at times another way according to how you feel on any given day.* (Galatians 5:17)

Remember, because we're born as sinners, we've developed habits of sin while growing up. Jay Adams said, "We were born sinners, but it took practice to develop our particular styles of sinning. The old life was disciplined [trained] toward ungodliness."[2] So now we're just doing what we've practiced for so long—sinning.

Have you ever broken your leg? The doctors put your leg in a cast and you don't get to use it for six weeks or so. When you get the cast off, you can't immediately return to doing everything you did before you broke it. If you're a skier or a skater, you'll probably need to go to rehab and gradually ease back into the expert slopes or triple jumps. It's going to take practice to get back to where you were.

Christians tend to sin out of habit. We've grown up as sinners and that's all we know how to do. It seems natural to lie, cheat, and steal. It feels okay to check out pornographic websites. It feels fine if we steal music online. It seems natural because it's the kind of thing we've grown up doing. All we know how to do is live for ourselves. We don't know how to live for God. When we first become Christians, are we expected to stop this overnight? What happens is that we spend the rest of our lives in rehab, learning how to live a new life.

Not only that, but also we live in a world filled with other sinners. The world around us screams, "It's okay! You're normal. Don't worry about it." The world tries to convince us that we don't need to change. In fact, it often encourages us to keep on sinning.

When we accept Christ, even though sin no longer has control of us, it still kicks around and tries to regain control. It uses guerrilla warfare and attempts to throw us off. We're delivered from sin but not from its attacks. If we don't keep it in check, sin easily turns our

- natural instincts into lust
- natural appetites into indulgence
- need for clothing and shelter into materialism
- normal sexual interest into immorality

Now you can see why Paul said not to "give sin a vote in the way you conduct your lives" (Romans 6:12). He knew that sin could control us, but he also knew that we have the power to stop it. Before Christ, we couldn't help but sin. We didn't know any better. But after Christ came into our life, our eyes were opened so we could distinguish the darkness of sin from the light of righteousness. Now that we're dead to sin—to its rule and reign—we can stand up to sin and say no. When we sin as Christians, we don't sin as slaves but as individuals with freedom of choice. We sin because we choose to sin.

We can wrap up all of this by remembering that God has made a way for us to be holy. Because of what Christ did on the cross, we've been freed from sin's control and we can now resist it. The responsibility is ours—we must resist sin. God doesn't do that for us. If we confuse the potential for resisting sin (which God provides) with the responsibility for resisting sin (which is our job), we invite sin into our lives. To chase after holiness, we have to understand this.

CHAPTER SIX

THE BATTLE FOR HOLINESS

The moment I decide to do good, sin is there to trip me up.

—ROMANS 7:21

Because of our relationship with Christ, we're free from the control of sin. But sin still puts up a pretty good fight.

Paul summed it up best: "The moment I decide to do good, sin is there to trip me up" (Romans 7:21). The fact that we'll live with this struggle for the rest of our earthly lives isn't the best news, is it? But if we realize what's going on and accept it—that is, if we acknowledge the sin that lives within us—we'll be able to fight against it better.

We've discussed those two opposing forces wrestling around inside of us—the nature that we have to sin and the desire to live a holy life (see 1 John 3:9). That's the picture Paul painted in Romans 7:21, and it distinguishes people who know Christ and want to chase after holiness from those who are unbelievers and are content to live in darkness.

We learned in chapter 5 that sin is still in us even though it doesn't have control anymore. However, even though it's been overthrown and weakened, its nature hasn't changed. Sin is still hostile to God and can't submit to his law (see Romans 8:7). As a result, we have an enemy living in our midst—in fact, right in our own heart. We've got to be on the watch constantly, because sin is ready to make sure we don't come out ahead. It wants us to fail.

What do you do if you're in a war? You come up with a battle plan. Let's see if we can do that with sin.

First, the Bible says that sin lives in the heart. "It's what comes out of a person that pollutes: obscenities, lusts, thefts, murders, adulteries, greed, depravity, deceptive dealings, carousing, mean looks, slander, arrogance, foolishness—all these are vomit from the heart. *There* is the source of your pollution" (Mark 7:20-23; see also Genesis 6:5 and Luke 6:45).

"Heart" is used in a lot of ways in the Bible. Sometimes it refers to our reason or understanding, sometimes to our affections and emotions, and sometimes to our will. Usually, though, it refers to the whole soul of a person and all its abilities working together in doing good or evil. The mind as it reasons, discerns, and judges; the emotions as they like or dislike; the conscience as it determines and warns; and the will as it chooses or refuses—all of these together are called the "heart."[1]

The Bible says the heart can be totally deceitful—no one but God can search and know it (see Jeremiah 17:9-10). We don't even know our own hearts (see 1 Corinthians 4:3-5). No one can know the hidden motives or the secrets of the way the heart works. The heart is where sin lives and where it gets most of its strength. We can't understand it—it remains hidden from us.

The heart is so deceitful that it makes up excuses, rationalizes, and justifies our actions. It keeps us blind to areas where sin is in contol. Sometimes our deceitful hearts will let us deal with sin part of the way, but then we get cut off. Or our hearts tell us that if we admit that a sin is a sin, just admitting it is as good as obeying God (see James 1:22).

It's a little scary to realize that sin can hide in our hearts. It means that we can't fully trust ourselves. So we have to ask God to search our hearts and reveal sin to us. This was David's prayer:

> *Investigate my life, O God,*
>> *find out everything about me;*
> *Cross-examine and test me,*
>> *get a clear picture of what I'm about;*
> *See for yourself whether I've done anything wrong —*
>> *then guide me on the road to eternal life.* (Psalm 139:23-24)

Okay, we want God to search our heart, but how does he do that? Through his Word, when we read it under the Holy Spirit's guidance. "His powerful Word is sharp as a surgeon's scalpel, cutting through everything, whether doubt or defense, laying us open to listen and obey. Nothing and no one is impervious to God's Word. We can't get away from it—no matter what" (Hebrews 4:12-13).

We have to let the Holy Spirit do the searching. If we don't, it's easy to fall into a couple of different traps. The first is the trap of constantly evaluating ourselves. This can easily become Satan's tool. One of his chief weapons is discouragement. He knows that if he can make us discouraged and dispirited, we'll stop the chase for holiness. The second trap is that of missing the real issues in our lives. Satan—along with our hearts—will let us focus on secondary issues.

I remember a friend who came to talk to me about a sin in his life. He just couldn't gain control over it. He was right about this problem area, but he was totally blind to other areas of sin in his life. The sin that he saw was mostly hurting only himself. But the problems he didn't or couldn't see were hurting others every day.

Only the Holy Spirit can help us see our blind spots.

We also need to realize that the sin in our lives works mostly through our desires. Ever since the Garden of Eden, we've listened to our desires more than our reasoning or logic. The next time you face one of your typical temptations, watch for the struggle between your desires and your reason. If you give in to temptation, it will be because desire has overcome reason in the struggle to influence your will. Believe it or not, you face this every day. The advertising and entertainment industries—among other influences—make appeals to our desires through what the writer of Hebrews called the pleasures of sin (see Hebrews 11:25).

Not all desire is evil, of course. Paul talked about his desire to know Christ personally (see Philippians 3:10), his desire for the salvation of his fellow Jews (see Romans 10:1), and the desire that his spiritual children would grow to maturity (see Galatians 4:19).

However, we're speaking here about desires that lead us into sin. Listen to what James said: "The temptation to give in to evil comes from us and only us. We have no one to blame but the leering, seducing flare-up of our own lust. Lust gets pregnant, and has a baby: sin! Sin grows up to adulthood, and becomes a real killer" (James 1:14-15). If we're going to win the war against sin, we have to get it through our thick heads that the problem is within us. Our own evil desires lead us into temptation.

You probably think that sin comes from outside you—you face a tempting situation and you just can't control yourself. Think again! The truth is, the evil desires within us are constantly looking for ways to satisfy their insatiable lusts. Think about the particular temptations that usually trip you up. How often do you find yourself looking for ways to satisfy those evil desires?

Sin stinks. It's so tricky that even when we're fighting against a particular sin, our sinful nature will try to trick us into playing with that very sin. We might even be in the middle of praying about or confessing a sin, and we'll start to dwell on the evil thoughts associated with that sin. The cycle starts over, and we're tempted again and then we find ourselves sinning again.

At other times, temptation pops up unexpectedly. Sin pounces at those times—and our sin nature is ready, willing, and able to go at a moment's notice. Think about wildfires that start as a spark but burn quickly through thousands of acres of forest land. If there's dry wood around and you bring the smallest bit of fire to it, it's going up in flames. Our sin nature and the temptations we face are exactly like that. Poof!

And here's another thing sin does—it lies to our understanding. Our reason, brought into the light by the Holy Spirit through the Word of God, stands in the way of sin gaining an upper hand through our desires. Satan's great strategy is to deceive us. Paul spoke of the "deceitful desires" of the old self (Ephesians 4:22, NIV). He said that we were at one time "stupid and stubborn, dupes of sin, ordered every which way by our glands" (Titus 3:3). These passages speak about our old life—before we came to know Christ personally. But this lie still wages war within us, even though it no longer controls us.

This whole thing with the mind happens a little bit at a time. If it happened fast, we might notice what's going on and try to resist it. Check out what God said about Ephraim:

> *Strangers suck him dry*
> > *but he doesn't even notice.*
> *His hair has turned gray—*
> > *he doesn't notice. (Hosea 7:9)*

That's exactly what happens to us! We're slowly drawn away from watching out for sin because we become overconfident. We believe we've conquered something when we really haven't. We look at the ways our friends are sinning and say, "I'd never do that!" But Paul warned us, "Don't be so naive and self-confident. You're not exempt. You could fall flat on your face as easily as anyone else" (1 Corinthians 10:12-13). Even when helping a fallen friend, we have to watch our step—we could be next (see Galatians 6:1).

Sometimes we can be drawn away by abusing God's grace. Jude spoke of certain men whose "design is to replace the sheer grace of our God with sheer license—which means doing away with Jesus Christ, our one and only Master" (Jude 1:4). How do we abuse grace?

- We abuse grace when we think we can sin and then receive forgiveness by claiming 1 John 1:9.
- We abuse grace when, after sinning, we dwell on the compassion and mercy of God to the exclusion of his holiness and hatred of sin.

Finally, we fall into sin when we question what God says in his Word. This was Satan's first tactic with Eve (see Genesis 3:1-5). Just as he said to Eve, "You won't die!" so Satan whispers lies to us, saying, "It is just a little thing!" or "God won't care about that sin."

Sin doesn't control us anymore, but it still puts up a good fight. It wages guerrilla warfare against us. If we don't do anything about it, it can still win the immediate battle. We have to take care of our sin immediately and firmly. Once you smell something rotten, you've got to throw it out. If we give temptation any sort of open door, it slowly and surely leads us into sin. "Because the sentence against evil deeds is so long in coming, people in general think they can get by with murder" (Ecclesiastes 8:11).

We'll be fighting this battle for the rest of our lives on earth. Jesus said, "Stay alert; be in prayer so you don't wander into tempation without even knowing you're in danger" (Matthew 26:41). And Solomon warned us, "Keep vigilant watch over your heart; *that's* where life starts" (Proverbs 4:23). Don't let sin win the battle for your heart.

CHAPTER SEVEN

HELP IN THE DAILY BATTLE

You are dead to sin and alive to God. That's what Jesus did.

—ROMANS 6:11

Maybe we should do a little recap here.

Okay, let's start at the beginning. You were born. When you came onto the scene, you told a few lies, stole that candy bar from the corner store, and made a few other minor mistakes as you were growing up. You weren't perfect, but you weren't a serial killer, either. You had it fairly together—or so you thought!

Then you heard about this guy, Jesus. Someone told you that even though you haven't killed anyone, you've still royally messed up in God's eyes. You realized that it's true. You really liked what you heard about God's love and how Jesus gives you access to a relationship with God, but you didn't know what to do. You couldn't seem to stop messing up.

And then someone turns on the light for you. The same person who told you about Jesus tells you that God provides you with an out from sinning. When Jesus died on the cross and took your place, he was giving himself up for you. He died to sin, and that means sin can't control you any longer. Because Jesus lived a perfect life and you've accepted what he did for you, you've also died to sin. You're free from sin! You have to remember that—you can resist sin so it won't control you.

Of course, as you read in the last chapter, sin is still creeping around you. It's cheating. Remember, it's like a terrorist waging guerrilla warfare. Sin went underground and it's trying to make its way back out. Admit it — after chapter 5, you probably felt some hope, but then chapter 6 smacked reality right back into you. You're thinking, *What does it matter if Jesus won the war if I still have to deal with this sin-terrorism within me? I feel just as defeated as before!*

The answer doesn't seem practical, because you have to trust God with the way he works. If you really want to experience holiness in your everyday life, you have to accept the fact that God — in his infinite wisdom — allows this daily battle to go on within you. But he doesn't leave the fighting to you alone. Remember, he's already rescued you from the control of sin. Well, part of the rescue is giving you the ability to win your daily battles with sin.

Let's look at Romans 6:11 again. There's something in there that you need to grab hold of and believe. You're not only dead to sin, as you saw in chapter 5; you're also alive to God. At one point you were living in darkness, but now you've been brought into the light — into the kingdom of God! Paul said that we've become slaves of righteousness (see Romans 6:18). God doesn't leave us dangling somewhere in the middle. He takes us from under the control of sin and brings us under the control of his Son.

You may be asking yourself: *What's the big deal about being alive to God? What help is it to me as I chase after holiness?* For starters, it means we're united with Jesus in all his power. You can't live a holy life on your own. Christianity is not a do-it-yourself thing.

Check out Paul's attitude in Philippians 4:11-13:

Actually, I don't have a sense of needing anything personally. I've learned by now to be quite content whatever my circumstances. I'm just as happy with little as with much, with much as with little. I've found the recipe for being happy whether full or hungry, hands full or hands empty. Whatever I have, wherever I am, I can make it through anything in the One who makes me who I am.

Paul was saying that he'd learned to be content no matter what circumstances he found himself in. If you've ever wondered how you were going to pay for a gallon of milk for your table or a gallon of gas for your car, you probably wonder, "How could Paul feel that way?" Paul answered the question — he was content because of the work of Christ, who ultimately gave him strength.

How does this apply to holiness? Your reactions to circumstances are a part of your walk of holiness. Remember, holiness isn't about a list of do's and don'ts. It's all about listening to God — following a new Master and obeying his will. Accepting with contentment whatever circumstances God allows for you is part of a holy walk.

You have to pay attention here — Paul said that he could be content because Christ gave him the ability to be content. Paul prayed a similar prayer for the Colossians:

We pray that you'll have the strength to stick it out over the long haul — not the grim strength of gritting your teeth but the glory-strength God gives. It is strength that endures the unendurable and spills over into joy, thanking the Father who makes us strong enough to take part in everything bright and beautiful that he has for us. (Colossians 1:11-12)

Where do the patience and power to endure come from? God. This is a recurring theme with Paul. In his letter to the Ephesians, he prayed, "I ask him to strengthen you by his Spirit—not a brute strength but a glorious inner strength—that Christ will live in you as you open the door and invite him in" (Ephesians 3:16-17). At the conclusion of that prayer, he prayed, "God can do anything, you know—far more than you could ever imagine or guess or request in your wildest dreams! He does it not by pushing us around but by working within us, his Spirit deeply and gently within us" (Ephesians 3:20).

Really then, this is the first thing we should grasp about being "alive to God." We're in a relationship with the One who's at work in us to give us strength with his power.

You've probably gone through times when you've felt completely out of control when it comes to a certain sin in your life. You've prayed about it, told others about it, and tried your hardest. But it still trips you up. It seems hopeless. On top of all that, Satan tells you, "You might as well give up. You can't beat that sin." And the sad fact is, the devil is right. On your own, you can't. But remember, you're alive to God and in a relationship with the One who gives you strength! This fact will provide the strength you need to fight your sin.

We have to realize that we're dead to sin. It can't control us. And on the flip side of that, we're alive to God. The One who gives us strength will help us. We then have the strength to keep sin from controlling us.

A famous Bible teacher, Dr. D. Martyn Lloyd-Jones, said,

To realize this takes away from us that old sense of hopelessness
which we have all known and felt because of the terrible power

of sin. . . . How does it work? It works in this way: I lose my
sense of hopelessness because I can say to myself that not only
am I no longer under the dominion of sin, but I am under the
dominion of another power that nothing can frustrate. However
weak I may be, it is the power of God that is working in me.[1]

This isn't just food for your head. If you want to keep sin from controlling you, you have to keep this fact at the front of your mind and deep in your heart—that "[fill in your name] is alive to God and dead to sin." Write it down, post it on your mirror, or put it up in your locker. Put it where you'll see it every day!

Getting beyond the hopeless cycle of sin will take more than memorizing, though. You also need to form the habit of continually realizing that you are dead to sin and alive to God. How do you do that? You put your faith in God's Word and you practice resisting sin's advances and temptations. You count on the fact that every time you're tempted, Christ will give you the strength you need to resist temptation and beat back the sin.

Don't forget that God gives us the Holy Spirit to live within us. When you enter into a relationship with Jesus, the Holy Spirit enters you—it's kind of like a mark he places on you to identify you as his child. What does the Holy Spirit do? He gives you spiritual life and the strength to live that life (see Romans 8:9-11). The Holy Spirit also works in you so that you can decide and act according to God's plans (see Philippians 2:13).

Paul said, "God has called us to be holy, not to live impure lives. Anyone who refuses to live by these rules is not disobeying human rules but is rejecting God, who gives his Holy Spirit to you" (1 Thessalonians

4:7-8, NLT). Paul connected the giving of the Holy Spirit with living a holy life. The Holy Spirit helps conform us to the character of God. This connection, the Holy Spirit and a holy life, is found in other passages as well.

> In sexual sin we violate the sacredness of our own bodies, these bodies that were made for God-given and God-modeled love, for "becoming one" with another. Or didn't you realize that your body is a sacred place, the place of the Holy Spirit?
> (1 Corinthians 6:18-19)

> For you who welcome [the Spirit of Christ], in whom he dwells—you yourself experience life on God's terms. . . . When God lives and breathes in you (and he does, as surely as he did in Jesus), you are delivered from that dead life. With his Spirit living in you, your body will be as alive as Christ's!
> (Romans 8:10-11)

> I advise you to live according to your new life in the Holy Spirit. Then you won't be doing what your sinful nature craves. (Galatians 5:16, NLT)

Why do you have the Holy Spirit living within you to give you strength to live a holy life? Because you're alive to God. You now live under God's reign. He unites you to Christ and gives you the Holy Spirit to live within you.[2]

The Holy Spirit gives us strength to live in holiness by opening our eyes and showing us that we need to be holy. He also helps us understand in new ways, and we begin to see God's standard of holiness. Then he causes us to become aware of specific areas of sin. One of

Satan's most powerful weapons is making us spiritually blind—unable to see our sinful character. The Bible says, "The heart is hopelessly dark and deceitful, a puzzle that no one can figure out" (Jeremiah 17:9). No one can understand it and expose it except the Holy Spirit.

Christians can even be deceived about their sins when they're reading the Bible or listening to someone teach from the Bible. I'm not sure how this happens, but we somehow feel that if we agree with what the Bible says, that's the same as obeying what the Bible says. We may get a point in a message, a book, or the Bible and say, "Totally. I believe that. I need to work on that." But then we let it drop there. James got straight to the point:

> Don't fool yourself into thinking that you are a listener when you are anything but, letting the Word go in one ear and out the other. Act on what you hear! Those who hear and don't act are like those who glance in the mirror, walk away, and two minutes later have no idea who they are, what they look like. (James 1:22-24)

As you grow in your faith, you'll also face the danger of spiritual pride. What's that? It's when you know what's right and wrong but you fail to see where your own character is lacking. Maybe you don't see your critical and unforgiving spirit or how you gossip or judge others. You may become like the Laodiceans. Jesus said this about them in the book of Revelation: "You make me want to vomit. You brag, 'I'm rich, I've got it made, I need nothing from anyone,' oblivious that in fact you're a pitiful, blind beggar, threadbare and homeless" (Revelation 3:16-17).

If you don't believe you can fall victim to spiritual pride, check out what happened to David. God called him "a man after his own heart." David had a lot going for him and was probably pretty far down the spiritual growth path. But he committed adultery with Bathsheba and then had her husband murdered to cover up the sin of adultery (see 2 Samuel 11). Did he come clean with God after that? Nope. Instead, he severely judged another man—wanting to put him to death—for a crime that wasn't half as bad as his own (see 2 Samuel 12:5). David was spiritually blind. It took Nathan the prophet to say, "You are the man!" before David could see how horrible his crime was.

The Holy Spirit will open your eyes to the reality of your inner life—to the fact that you're totally sinful and there's nothing you can do on your own to change that. The Holy Spirit says to us, "You are the man!" or "You are the woman!" Even if that message comes from the lips of another Christian who loves us, it's the Holy Spirit who opens our eyes and allows us to see the truth. At that point, you can join David and say, "I have sinned against the Lord." Once you open your eyes and begin to honestly look at yourself, you'll know that the Holy Spirit is working in you. This is where he begins his ministry of making us holy.

When your eyes are open, when you see God's standard and your own sinfulness, something will start to change in you—you'll start to desire holiness. This is another ministry of the Holy Spirit as he works to make us holy. "For God can use sorrow in our lives to help us turn away from sin and seek salvation. We will never regret that kind of sorrow. But sorrow without repentance is the kind that results in death" (2 Corinthians 7:10, NLT).

The Holy Spirit helps us turn back to God. You can say with David,

I know how bad I've been;
  My sins are staring me down.

You're the One I've violated, and you've seen
  it all, seen the full extent of my evil. . . .

Soak me in your laundry and I'll come out clean,
  scrub me and I'll have a snow-white life. (Psalm 51:3-4,7)

Paul said, "It is God who works in you to will and to act according to his good purpose" (Philippians 2:13, NIV). Before we can act, we must will. To "will" means to have a desire or resolve to change. When the Holy Spirit shows you your sinfulness, he doesn't do so to lead you into despair. He wants to lead you toward holiness. How does that happen? First, he creates a hatred of your sins and then he places a desire for holiness in you.

At this point, you're probably saying, "This is going to be a lot harder and take a lot more time than I thought. If I'm really going to chase after holiness, I really need to want it. It can't be a passing fad, here one day and gone the next. I'm going to fail a lot. Satan is going to attack me and never let up, and my own sins will keep kicking around within me." But I hope you'll also pray, "I trust and know that the Holy Spirit is at work within me and that he will continue to create a desire for holiness, and I will continue to chase after it."

You must be getting this by now: the Holy Spirit creates this desire, not only by showing you your sins, but also by showing you God's standard of holiness. The primary way he does this is through the Bible. As you read and study Scripture or hear it taught, you'll be amazed by God's standard of holiness. Even though his standard may seem far beyond what you're capable of, you can recognize and respond to that which is "holy, righteous and good" (Romans 7:12, NIV). Even though you may fail a lot, in your inner being you will "delight in God's law" (Romans 7:22, NIV).

So here's another point to think about between what God does and what you must do. If the Holy Spirit uses the Bible to show you your need and to bring a desire for holiness, it should seem pretty logical that you need to be reading the Bible regularly. You should approach the Bible or a biblical message at church with the prayer that the Holy Spirit would search your heart for any sin in you (see Psalm 139:23-24).

After the Holy Spirit has opened your eyes so that you see your need and has created a desire for holiness within you, he still has something more to do. He must give you the spiritual strength to live a holy life. Paul said, "I advise you to live according to your new life in the Holy Spirit. Then you won't be doing what your sinful nature craves" (Galatians 5:16, NLT). Living by the Spirit means living both in obedience to and dependence on the Holy Spirit. There's a balance between our will (when we obey God) and our faith (when we depend on God for strength). Right now, though, we're looking at the second part, depending on the Holy Spirit.

You depend on the Holy Spirit because you simply can't overcome your sinfulness on your own. You need the strength of the Holy Spirit. Peter said that God has given us "the best invitation we ever received! We were also given absolutely terrific promises to pass on to you— your tickets to participation in the life of God after you turned your back on a world corrupted by lust" (2 Peter 1:3-4).

You can express your dependence on the Holy Spirit for a holy life in two ways:

1. Through a humble and consistent intake of Scripture.

- If you really want to live in the realm of the Spirit, you have to continually feed your mind with his truth. It's hypocritical to pray for victory over your sins yet totally neglect your intake of God's Word, his basic means of communicating with you.
- When you do this, you need to be dependent on the Holy Spirit. God says, "I will bless those who have humble and contrite hearts, who tremble at my word" (Isaiah 66:2, NLT). You need to come to the Word with this attitude because you acknowledge the fact that you're sinful. Most of the time we're blind to that, and we need to study the Bible knowing that the power of the Holy Spirit will open our eyes again.

2. By praying for holiness. The apostle Paul was praying all the time for the working of God's Spirit in the people he was writing to.

- He told the Ephesians that he prayed that God would "strengthen you by his Spirit—not a brute strength but a glorious inner strength" (Ephesians 3:16).
- For the Colossians, he prayed God would "give you a complete understanding of what he wants to do in your lives, and we ask him to make you wise with spiritual wisdom" so that they "will always honor and please the Lord, and you will continually do good, kind things for others. All the while, you will learn to know God better and better" (Colossians 1:9-10, NLT).
- He wrote to the Thessalonians, "May God himself, the God who makes everything holy and whole, make you holy and whole, put you together—spirit, soul, and body—and keep you fit for the coming of our Master, Jesus Christ" (1 Thessalonians 5:23).

- And he also told the Thessalonians, "May the Lord make your love grow and overflow to each other and to everyone else, just as our love overflows toward you. As a result, Christ will make your hearts strong, blameless, and holy when you stand before God our Father" (1 Thessalonians 3:12-13, NLT).

Paul knew that we need to depend on the Holy Spirit for holiness, and he showed us this dependence through the prayers he prayed.

When you first became a Christian, you probably figured that you had the answer to the sin in your life. All you needed to do was get into the Bible and follow what it told you to do. You probably did that for a while (as best as you could), but then it became way too hard.

You can't do this thing called the Christian life on your own. What you need to do is fess up and realize that only through the power of the Holy Spirit are you able to make any progress. If you make gains toward living a holy life, it starts because of what the Holy Spirit is doing in you, not anything you're doing on your own. After a while, you'll look to him and see that he's been revealing your sin, creating a desire for holiness, and giving you the strength to respond to him in obedience.

CHAPTER EIGHT

OBEDIENCE, NOT VICTORY

*Dear brothers and sisters, you have no obligation whatsoever
to do what your sinful nature urges you to do. For if you keep
on following it, you will perish. But if through the power of the
Holy Spirit you turn from it and its evil deeds, you will live.*

—ROMANS 8:12-13, NLT

Now we get to the fun part—our responsibility.

It's clear from Romans 8:12-13 that God puts responsibility for living a holy life directly on us. We're supposed to do something. We're not supposed to "stop trying and start trusting"; we're to turn from our sins. Paul and other writers told us over and over that we need to take the responsibility for living a holy life. Paul said, "That means killing off everything connected with that way of death" (Colossians 3:5).

The writer of Hebrews said, "Do you see what this means—all these pioneers who blazed the way, all these veterans cheering us on? It means we'd better get on with it. Strip down, start running—and never quit!" (Hebrews 12:1). As you chase after holiness, how could the words of this writer be any clearer? It's our responsibility to run the Christian race. James said, "Let God work his will in you. Yell a loud *no* to the Devil and watch him scamper" (James 4:7). Even here we take action—yelling no to the Devil. Peter said, "Do your very best to be found living at your best, in purity and peace" (2 Peter 3:14). The clause "do your very best" addresses our wills. It is something we must decide to do.

Think about these verses:

- "The Spirit can make life. Sheer muscle and willpower don't make anything happen" (John 6:63).
- "I need to emphasize, friends, that our natural, earthly lives don't in themselves lead us by their very nature into the kingdom of God" (1 Corinthians 15:50).

From these verses, it might be easy to think that we can't (or shouldn't) do anything on our own efforts to chase after holiness. The Bible seems to be saying that it's all about God and the Holy Spirit—we can just sit back, relax, and let God do the work for us.

But if you look back at the verses we've covered before, you'll recall that it's a joint effort. We can't do it alone, and God chooses not to do it all for us.

So because we have the Holy Spirit in us, we can't say, "I fell into sin" or "I was tempted and gave in to sin." Get real! If we sin, it's because we choose to sin, not because we can't say no to the temptation.

We need to face up to our own responsibility for holiness. If we say, "I fell into sin," we make it sound as though a hole suddenly appeared before us and we couldn't avoid falling into it. Maybe the reality is that we've fallen, but it wasn't a surprise, and it certainly didn't appear out of nowhere. Usually we've been tempted along the way. The "falling" is really just the moment when we give in to the temptation.

We need to stand up to our responsibility for our thoughts, attitudes, and actions. We need to acknowledge that we died to the control of sin—we're not under its power anymore. We need to realize that God gave his Son to us, whose power we have through the Holy

Spirit. If we accept this responsibility, then we'll start to make progress in our chase for holiness.

CHAPTER NINE

PUTTING SIN TO DEATH

> *That means killing off everything connected with that way of death: sexual promiscuity, impurity, lust, doing whatever you feel like whenever you feel like it, and grabbing whatever attracts your fancy.* —COLOSSIANS 3:5

So far, it's pretty clear that holiness is our responsibility. If we're going to chase after holiness, we need to come to a decision that we'll do the work we need to do.

Maybe you know someone (or maybe it's you) who's stuck in a particular sin. Perhaps if we don't want to make the effort to stop, we'll pray for God to motivate us to stop the sin. That's like saying that God hasn't already done enough for us and we need him to do one more thing. When we do that, it just delays our facing up to our own responsibility for living a holy life.

What's that responsibility? We need to put our sins to death (see Romans 8:13). In Colossians 3:3,5, Paul said, "Your old life is dead. . . . And that means killing off everything connected with that way of death." It is obvious what we're supposed to do. We need to cut off any life—the very blood supply—we give to the sins that ruled our lives before Christ.

If only it were as easy as killing off the enemy in a video game. You sit down, take the controller in hand, and fire away. You can see who and what the enemy is, and all you have to do is pull the trigger. It's not like that with sin. We can't do it by ourselves, and remember, sin often goes underground, so we don't see it. We need the Holy Spirit to help us. Only the strength of the Holy Spirit can help us kill off the sins of our old life.

So now you know *what* you must do. The important question to ask next is, *how* do I cut off the power of the sins controlling me? If you're even going to attempt this extreme challenge, you need to be sure that you really want to do this. Why? Because you can't go into this half-heartedly—you have to give it everything you've got. You have to believe that chasing after a holy life is important to you. You must be convinced that the stress and strain of the chase are worth the effort and the pain required to kill off your old life of sin. You must believe that "without holiness no one will see the Lord" (Hebrews 12:14, NIV).

Not only do you need to develop the belief that a holy life is important, but you also have to develop convictions in specific areas of obedience. These convictions come from being in God's Word.

We've explored what the Bible says quite a bit. But during most of our lives, our minds are filled with the world's values. Even after we become Christians, the world around us constantly tries to get us to do what it wants us to. We're surrounded by temptations to give in to sin. That's why Paul said, "Don't become so well-adjusted to your culture that you fit into it without even thinking" (Romans 12:2).

Only by God's Word will our minds be remolded and our values renewed. When God gave instructions for future kings of Israel, he said, "That scroll is to remain at his side at all times; he is to study it every day so that he may learn what it means to fear his GOD, living in reverent obedience before these rules and regulations by following them" (Deuteronomy 17:19). The king was supposed to read God's law his whole life so he could learn the necessity of holiness and how to know God's will in various situations.

Jesus said, "The person who knows my commandments and keeps them, that's who loves me" (John 14:21). Obedience is the pathway to holiness, but we can obey God's commands only if we know them. We must give God's Word such a prominent place in our minds that it becomes the biggest influence on our thoughts, our attitudes, and our actions.

One of the most effective ways of influencing our minds is by memorizing Scripture. One psalmist said, "I've banked your promises in the vault of my heart so I won't sin myself bankrupt" (Psalm 119:11). Of course, the purpose of memorizing Scripture is to apply it. You need to use the verses you study and memorize. Doing this every day will help you develop the kind of conviction you need to help you avoid the sins you usually get caught up in.

The Bible clearly addresses many life issues, and it's good to memorize verses about those issues. For example, God's will concerning honesty is clear: "No more lies, no more pretense. Tell your neighbor the truth. In Christ's body we're all connected to each other, after all. When you lie to others, you end up lying to yourself" (Ephesians 4:25). His will concerning abstinence from sexual immorality is also plain: "Keep yourselves from sexual promiscuity. Learn to appreciate and give dignity to your body, not abusing it, as is so common among those who know nothing of God" (1 Thessalonians 4:3-5). It shouldn't be hard to develop convictions about God's will concerning these clearly stated issues if we're willing to obey his Word.

But what about issues that aren't mentioned specifically in the Bible—how do we determine God's will and develop conviction in those areas?

Some people use a formula called "How to Know Right from Wrong." When you run across an issue that you don't think the Bible defines clearly, you can use these four questions based on three verses in 1 Corinthians:

- Is it helpful to my spirit, mind, and health? "Just because something is technically legal doesn't mean that it's spiritually appropriate" (6:12).
- Does it control me? "If I went around doing whatever I thought I could get by with, I'd be a slave to my whims" (6:12).
- Does it hurt others? "Never go to these idol-tainted meals if there's any chance it will trip up one of your brothers or sisters" (8:13).
- Does it glorify God? "Do everything that way, heartily and freely to God's glory" (10:31).

I don't really like formulas, and this one seems almost too simple. But if you're serious about chasing after holiness, these questions will be much deeper and tougher and more searching than you might imagine. We need to keep asking these questions if we really want to make holiness a part of our everyday life.

Let's think about these principles in some typical situations. Think about the movies or TV shows you watch. Are they appropriate or helpful in your life? If they aren't, maybe you need to think about not watching them anymore.

What about the question "Does it control me?" Maybe your initial thought is about drugs, smoking, or drinking. Obviously those things can involve addiction, which is control. But there can also be other things that may not seem like control issues to you. Maybe you're a perfectionist at school. Or maybe you're obsessed with your boyfriend or girlfriend. Perhaps food or sports or work has control over your life. It's important to realize that while the activity itself may not be sinful, when we make it an idol in our lives, it becomes sin.

Think about the next question, "Does it hurt others?" It is possible for you to do something that's not a sin for you but could be a sin for someone else. For example, maybe you decide that a certain TV show isn't inappropriate for you to watch, but your friend really struggles with sin issues in that show. For you to watch the show in the presence of that friend could cause him to sin. Just because it's not sin for you doesn't mean that other people won't struggle with it. Be careful not to set others up for sin.

But what about areas where Christians disagree about God's will? Paul addressed this in Romans 14 where he talked about the problem of eating certain foods. He gave us three principles to help us when Christians don't agree:

1. Don't judge others whose beliefs are different from your own (see verses 1-4).
2. Whatever your convictions are, develop them out of obedience to God (see verses 5-8).
3. Whatever your convictions are, be true to them (see verse 23).

If we go against what we believe—what God convicts us is right— we're actually sinning. That's true even if others don't face that same sin issue.

Here's where it gets serious. If you're chasing after holiness, you need to ask, "Am I willing to develop convictions or beliefs from the Bible—and live by those beliefs?" This is tough. We often hesitate to face up to God's standard of holiness in a specific area of life. Why?

Because if we're going to follow that standard, we have to be obedient. And we may not be willing to do that.

This brings us to another quality we need to develop if we want to kill off the sins of our old life. That quality is commitment. Jesus said, "Simply put, if you're not willing to take what is dearest to you, whether plans or people, and kiss it good-bye, you can't be my disciple" (Luke 14:33). We need to honestly face the question, "Am I willing to give up a certain habit that keeps me from holiness?" Most of us fail right at this point of commitment. Sometimes we just dabble in sin by doing it a little without getting too deeply involved. Or maybe you're like a lot of people—you try to break your life into pieces. When you're in certain places or with certain friends, you won't swear, but as soon as you're in a different setting (the car, for example) or with different friends, you can cuss like the proverbial sailor.

Other times, we suffer from the "just one more time" syndrome. We'll just go a little bit further next time, have sex one more time, go to that inappropriate Internet site once a month instead of every week. Each of these "just one more" moments keeps us from really making the commitment and saying "Enough!" to sin.

Solomon said, "Hell has a voracious appetite, and lust just never quits" (Proverbs 27:20). Whether it's stealing one more look at a pornographic website or repeating just one more juicy piece of gossip, it doesn't matter. The sin's appetite will never be satisfied. In fact, the opposite happens—every time we say yes, we make it harder to say no the next time.

Remember, we've developed habits of sin. Maybe we've developed the habit of twisting the truth a little when it helps us. Or we've developed the habit of taking (or downloading) things we haven't paid for.

We need to break these habits, but we can't unless we make a basic commitment to chase a life of holiness without exceptions.

The apostle John said, "I write this, dear children, to guide you out of sin" (1 John 2:1). The whole purpose of John's letter is that we not sin. One day as I was studying 1 John 2, I realized that my personal goal regarding holiness was far less than John's. In effect, he was saying, "Make it your aim not to sin." As I gave this some thought, I realized that deep within my heart my real aim was not to sin *very much*. I found it difficult to say, "Yes, Lord, from here on I will make it my aim not to sin *at all*." I realized that God was calling me that day to a deeper level of commitment to holiness than I'd ever been willing to make before.

Can you imagine a soldier going into battle with the aim of "not getting shot very much"? That's ridiculous, of course. He's doesn't want to get shot at all! If we don't make a commitment to chase after holiness *without exception*, we're just like a soldier going into battle with the aim of not getting shot very much. If that's our goal, we'll certainly be shot — not with bullets, but with temptation, over and over again.

Jonathan Edwards, one of the great preachers of early American history, used to make resolutions. One was "Resolved, never to do anything which I would be afraid to do if it were the last hour of my life."[1] Could you make that resolution your own? Are you willing to commit to the practice of holiness without exception? There's really no point in praying for victory over temptation if you're not willing to make a commitment to say no to it.

Only by learning to say no to temptation can we kill off the sin that controls our life. Learning this is slow and painful. We'll fail at times. Old habits die hard. But we have to keep on going if we want to succeed.

CHAPTER TEN

TRAINING FOR THE MARATHON

Stay clear of silly stories that get dressed up as religion.
Exercise daily in God—no spiritual flabbiness, please!

—1 TIMOTHY 4:7

Here's something that will probably disappoint you: even if you have strong convictions and have made a commitment to chase after holiness, you might still fail. You probably will. Think about it: maybe you make a conscious decision to stop gossiping or to stop thinking lustfully, but tomorrow you mess up and do it again. It's a pain to keep failing when you're really trying to succeed.

Think about our world of fast food and ATMs. Everything around us is instant. Naturally, we want the process of holiness to be quick and easy too. But just like training for a sport or learning an instrument, success doesn't come overnight. And it rarely comes without our making an effort. These things, like holiness, take practice and discipline.

In the context of our Christian faith, discipline sounds painful or boring. But think about it like you might work on training your body for a marathon. Who could just wake up one day and go out and run a marathon? Your body would need time and training to be conditioned for such a long run.

Discipline is like training or practicing for what lies ahead. Just as Paul said in 1 Timothy 4:7, "Exercise daily in God—no spiritual flabbiness, please!" We need to be active in our chase for holiness, and that involves exercise.

> You've all been to the stadium and seen the athletes race. Everyone runs; one wins. Run to win. All good athletes train hard. They do it for a gold medal that tarnishes and fades. You're after one that's gold eternally.
> I don't know about you, but I'm running hard for the finish line. I'm giving it everything I've got. No sloppy living for me! I'm staying alert and in top condition. (1 Corinthians 9:24-27)

Paul's enthusiasm about the chase is infectious, isn't it? If we want to become more holy, how can we stay in top condition? What does our training look like?

The best tool for our training is the Bible. Check out 2 Timothy 3:16: "Every part of Scripture is God-breathed and useful one way or another—showing us truth, exposing our rebellion, correcting our mistakes, training us to live God's way." It's been said before—the only way Scripture can be used to train us is if we actually read it. That's where it gets tough. The Holy Spirit can help us understand the Bible, but first we have to read it to learn what God wants for us. Once we learn what God wants, the Holy Spirit can help us remember those things for the times we need them. These reminders can help us say no whenever we're tempted.

The Bible, in our race, is like the carbs and protein a runner fills up with. It's the fuel we need to get through our race. If a marathon runner heads out on an empty stomach, she won't make it far before she collapses. If we don't want to collapse, we need to make healthy portions of the Bible a part of our regular diet as we train for the chase after holiness.

Of course, with so many other things fighting for our attention every day, most of us struggle to do that. Satan adds to the stress by helping us find excuses:

- It's too early; I'm tired.
- I have too much homework to do.
- It's too late; I'm tired.

This is where we need to bring discipline into play. If a runner gives up practicing for a few days, it will take him time to rebuild his stamina. If we aren't actively "exercising" our faith, we'll be weaker and more susceptible to sin.

But discipline means finding or making time to get into the Bible. Whenever is best for you, just do it. If you're a morning person, get up a little earlier to read your Bible before you go to work or school. If you're a night owl, stay up a little later than usual to read before you go to sleep. If you have a break in the middle of the day from school or work, stop to read. Just make sure you make time to do it.

The thing about reading the Bible to exercise our faith, though, is that we have to really take in what we read. We can't just look at it. We have to read it, think about it, pray about it, and live it. Sometimes it's also helpful to do a study (on our own or in a group). This can really help us get into the Word and understand what it means for our life.

This concept of "read, think, pray, and live" isn't new. For centuries, Christians have used a method of Bible reading called *lectio divina*. It sounds pretty lofty, but it's really all about these four words:

- Read—a passage or chapter of Scripture.
- Think—meditate on it, ponder it, focus on it.

- Pray—ask God to help you apply and understand it.
- Live—take what you're learning and live it out.

You don't even have to do all of these things in one chunk of time. If you have a few minutes in the morning to focus on the Bible, read it. During the rest of the day, look for opportunities to pray and meditate (think) about it. As you do this, you'll almost naturally find ways to apply it to your life. As you apply it, you'll be living what you learned.

While all of the *lectio* elements are important, they're a waste of time if you never actually take those last steps and apply what you learn to your everyday life. This is where we grow in holiness—as we apply God's lessons in our lives.

It's usually easy to start a new plan. The hard part is keeping it up. That's why, as we train for this chase, we need perseverance. Every time a runner beats his own time, she sees an opportunity to improve even more—but only if she stays in shape and keeps training. The same is true as we chase after holiness. We'll have failures and successes. But we need to keep training and keep chasing. That's the only way we'll grow.

The Bible provides plenty of examples of people failing. Paul said, "What I don't understand about myself is that I decide one way, but then I act another, doing things I absolutely despise" (Romans 7:15). Can you relate? As humans, it feels like we're constantly doing the wrong thing, even when we know what's right (and when we actually want to *do* what's right).

The good news is that God knows how we are, and he's there to help us. Proverbs says,

No matter how many times you trip them up,
    God-loyal people don't stay down long.
Soon they're up on their feet,
    while the wicked end up flat on their faces. (Proverbs 24:16)

God's Spirit will help us up when we're down. The Spirit will help us remember what we've learned from God's Word. Over time, we'll know and choose the right path. Even when we stray from the trail, the Spirit helps us look back and see the great life on the path, and we'll persevere to get back there. So when you fail, don't give up. Get back in the race and chase after your goal.

CHAPTER ELEVEN

HOLINESS IN BODY AND MIND

> *With promises like this to pull us on, dear friends, let's make a*
> *clean break with everything that defiles or distracts us, both*
> *within and without. Let's make our entire lives fit and holy*
> *temples for the worship of God.*   —2 CORINTHIANS 7:1

Maybe you've heard the saying "Garbage in, garbage out." Well, that thought is true for both our bodies and our minds. If we fill our bodies with things that are unhealthy, we won't be as strong and ready as necessary when temptation comes along. If we fill our minds with trash, we'll easily forget about things that are holy—and our lives will begin to display the trash we take in.

To really be holy, we need to have control over our bodies and our minds. If our bodies are temples for the Holy Spirit, we need to make sure they're a place fit for God.

This is a topic that has the possibility of sounding legalistic. But that's not what this is about at all. It's about balance. This concept can help us keep some control over the things that may become idols for us (food, alcohol, drugs) and the things that can lead us away from the chase (lustful thoughts, hatred, gossip).

Like our bodies, our thoughts can also have control over us. Paul said, "Summing it all up, friends, I'd say you'll do best by filling your minds and meditating on things true, noble, reputable, authentic, compelling, gracious—the best, not the worst; the beautiful, not the ugly; things to praise, not things to curse" (Philippians 4:8).

And while our negative thoughts can lead us into sin, sometimes our negative thoughts can *be* the sin. Remember, Jesus said, "I'm telling you that anyone who is so much as angry with a brother or sister is guilty of murder" (Matthew 5:22). That's pretty strong, but it's true. If we store away anger long enough, it could lead to murder—at least in our hearts. Maybe you've heard someone who is angry with another person say, "He's dead to me." It's as though the speaker has killed someone else off in his or her mind, because that's easier than dealing with anger toward the other. Jesus knew how powerful our thoughts can be.

Stay grounded in God's Word. That will help you find ways to fight off the negative things that try to invade your thoughts. And it will help you avoid the unhealthy things we all try to fill up on.

CHAPTER TWELVE

HOLINESS AND OUR WILLS

That energy is God's energy, an energy deep within you, God himself willing and working at what will give him the most pleasure. —PHILIPPIANS 2:13

Along with everything we've covered so far in the chase after holiness—conviction and commitment, perseverance and discipline, and holiness in body and mind—we need to remember that our wills are always involved. It's our will that makes the choice to obey or sin. The will determines whether we give in to temptation or resist it by saying no.

We've touched on the idea of will already. But because the will has so much control over our actions, it's smart to understand how it works. We also need to learn how to get our wills to submit to and obey God every day.

Our will works in conjunction with the rest of our soul (mind, emotions, and conscience). When God first created humans, our wills were in perfect harmony with God's will. But that was back in Eden—before the Fall. Once Adam and Eve gave in to sin, their unity with God in mind, spirit, and will was cut off. Because Adam and Eve represented all of us, we all lose that unity with God in mind, spirit, and will. That's why it can be so hard for us to obey God sometimes—because for thousands of years people have had wills that naturally go against God's will.

Whenever we decide to follow our will in the wrong direction, something usually compels us through either our reason (our mind) or our emotions (our heart). That's why we need to be careful of what we let into our minds and hearts. Solomon—the wise man who wrote the Proverbs—said, "Keep vigilant watch over your heart; *that's* where life starts" (Proverbs 4:23). If we keep good watch over what is in our hearts and minds, we'll be able to more clearly hear what God's will for us is.

So, how do we "keep vigilant watch" over our hearts? Let's see what God says in his Word:

- "How can a young person live a clean life? By carefully reading the map of your Word" (Psalm 119:9).
- "Tune your ears to the world of Wisdom; set your heart on a life of Understanding" (Proverbs 2:2).

These verses talk about how to guard our minds. In Proverbs we're told to tune in to wisdom. Where does true wisdom come from? The wisest one—God. And the psalm says that reading God's Word can help us keep a "clean life"—both in mind and in actions.

However, Satan has an incredible ability to attack us through our emotions, especially through the things we really want. Sometimes he'll attack our mind first so he can confuse us. Then, once we're unsure of the truth, he attacks by messing with our desires. That's what he did to Eve in the Garden of Eden. First he lied to her, contradicting the truth she knew from what God had told her. Satan said, "You won't die. God knows that the moment you eat from that tree, you'll see what's really going on"(Genesis 3:4-5). Once Eve started to doubt God's truth, Satan messed with her desires, upsetting her feelings of being content and encouraging her to be all-knowing, "You'll be just like God, knowing everything, ranging all the way from good to evil." Then she gave in (Genesis 3:5).

Because we know that Satan attacks us most often through our desires, we need to keep a sharp watch over those, too. We need to "pursue the things over which Christ presides. Don't shuffle along, eyes to the ground, absorbed with the things right in front of you. Look up, and be alert to what is going on around Christ—that's where the action is" (Colossians 3:1-2).

Sometimes it's easy to "get" something in our heads but not "feel" like doing it. We need some encouragement in those times, maybe some motivation from people who have gone before us. Check out Hebrews 11—the "Faith Hall of Fame." Reading the stories of these normal people who had to overcome their minds and emotions to do God's will can help you feel more confident doing that yourself. It can also be helpful to hang out with people who'll be honest with you when they see you struggling with an area of sin. Make sure you have friends who'll be honest enough to hold you accountable in the areas you're working on.

God's at work within us, helping us to do what pleases him. But at the same time, we have to work hard to guard our minds and emotions so that our wills line up with God's will. This is how we'll see the Holy Spirit helping us to become more holy.

CHAPTER THIRTEEN

HABITS OF HOLINESS

> *You can readily recall, can't you, how at one time the more you
> did just what you felt like doing — not caring about others, not
> caring about God — the worse your life became and the less
> freedom you had? And how much different is it now as you live
> in God's freedom, your lives healed and expansive in holiness?*
>
> —ROMANS 6:19

We've had this discussion about habits before, but let's focus on it more now. We've concluded that the more you sin, the easier it becomes to sin. It's like a habit you develop. It's like that old saying from Shakespeare, "O what a tangled web we weave, when first we practice to deceive." Basically, one lie leads to several others, crossing and tangling, and soon you can't see your way out of the web of lies.

Just as you can develop bad habits, or habits of sin, so you can also develop good habits, habits of holiness.

Before we were Christians, we were pretty good at developing bad habits. But our bad habits trapped us in a pattern of sin. Paul said, "You can readily recall, can't you, how at one time the more you did just what you felt like doing—not caring about others, not caring about God— the worse your life became and the less freedom you had?" (Romans 6:19). We were caught in sin, tangled and trapped in that giant web. But with Jesus, we have freedom from sin. "Sin can't tell you how to live" (Romans 6:14). So because we're free, we need to be sure that we don't allow ourselves to be caught up in our old bad habits anymore.

We kill off the bad habits by asking the Holy Spirit to point them out and help us get rid of them. We also need to ask the Holy Spirit to help us start some new, good habits.

There are four things you can remember as you work on new habits:

1. Do it over and over. Just as sinning makes it easier to sin more, so saying no to sin makes it easier to say no. Pay attention to the sins or temptations that keep coming to you. Pray for help to say no, then practice saying no. No to the drugs at that party. No to the prepackaged research paper online. No to whatever sin keeps coming after you.

2. Don't say, "Just this once." Remember, when you sin, it's easier to sin again. If you say, "Just this once. I'll stop [fill in the blank] tomorrow," you're pretty unlikely to stop tomorrow. Hold to your decisions.

3. Resist all sins, even the ones that "don't seem so bad." If you decide that you don't need to kill all of your bad habits, and you hold on to "little ones," you'll eventually decide that you can give in to a "bigger one."

4. Don't give up when you fail. We all fail from time to time. But if you give up trying, only that makes you a failure.

As you work on these four principles, you'll see some progress in your chase. It takes work to stop our bad habits and to start good ones. Be sure to ask the Holy Spirit to help you. It's what he's there for. This is how you'll go farther in your chase after holiness.

CHAPTER FOURTEEN

HOLINESS AND FAITH

By an act of faith, Abraham said yes to God's call to travel to an unknown place that would become his home. When he left he had no idea where he was going. —HEBREWS 11:8

Get ready to blush a little. As you chase after holiness, you might choose to do something that looks ridiculous to the rest of the world. But this would be good embarrassment!

A famous Christian musician made a significant amount of money, but he told his business manager to pay him what a factory worker from his town would be paid and to give the rest away to various ministries he supported. He never actually knew how much money he made. Imagine a Hollywood actor doing that. It's pretty hard to picture, especially in a world where actors fight for millions of dollars per episode or movie! But because God calls us to help those who don't have as much as we have, and because this musician didn't want money to become his god, he obeyed. Like Abraham did, this artist obeyed by faith what he believed to be God's will for him, even though it was probably tough to do sometimes.

Holiness isn't just about staying away from sin and bad habits. It's also about obeying God's will. We need to say, like Jesus did, "I'm here to do it your way, O God" (Hebrews 10:7). Obedience is key to our chase after holiness, no matter what it may be that God is calling us to do.

Most of us struggle with knowing God's will. Sure, it'd be a lot easier if we had some mystical way of hearing directly from God. But a lot of times, obedience is simply a step of faith. In fact, the book of Hebrews (see chapters 3 and 4) uses "faith" and "obedience" almost interchangeably.

The stories of the "heroes of faith" in Hebrews 11 also show how faith and obedience go hand in hand. These heroes obeyed by faith. They had to believe that doing what God wanted would be the best thing for them to do. Faith is believing in things we can't see. So, when they obeyed *by faith*, it was because they believed in God's plan, even if they didn't understand it or see the whole picture that God could see.

Check out some of the examples of faith from Hebrews 11:

By an act of faith, Abel brought a better sacrifice to God than Cain. It was what he believed, not what he brought, that made the difference. (verse 4)

By faith, Noah built a ship in the middle of dry land. He was warned about something he couldn't see, and acted on what he was told. The result? His family was saved. His act of faith drew a sharp line between the evil of the unbelieving world and the rightness of the believing world. As a result, Noah became intimate with God. (verse 7)

By an act of faith, Abraham said yes to God's call to travel to an unknown place that would become his home. When he left he had no idea where he was going. (verse 8)

The author of Hebrews says, "Each one of these people of faith died not yet having in hand what was promised, but still believing. How did they do it?" (11:13). The answer is that they trusted and believed in God's promises to them. They continued to have faith in things they couldn't see.

Don't let anyone fool you. The chase after holiness is a tough race to run, especially when it comes to obedience. You have to have conviction (belief) in the necessity of obeying God's will as well as confidence (faith) in God's promises. If you don't have both of those, you can't persevere in this difficult chase.

Think again about Eve in the garden. Apparently, she didn't have a complete conviction that she should *always* obey God, and she didn't have confidence in what he told her. Because she lacked faith, she disobeyed. The Bible contains plenty of other stories like that. That's one of the beauties of Scripture—God shows us the failures of people as well as their successes so we can learn from them.

Is there anything in your life that you know God is calling you to do, but you choose not to—because you lack either conviction or confidence? Can you imagine what your life would look like if you trusted and obeyed God?

"It's impossible to please God apart from faith. And why? Because anyone who wants to approach God must believe both that he exists *and* that he cares enough to respond to those who seek him" (Hebrews 11:6). If we're going to chase after holiness, we must have faith to obey the will of God and faith to believe that God will give us what he promises.

CHAPTER FIFTEEN

HOLINESS IN AN UNHOLY WORLD

I'm not asking that you take them out of the world but that you guard them from the Evil One. —JOHN 17:15

Every Christian lives in the context of an unholy world. Some areas are worse than others, like some college campuses where partying is more important than studying, businesses where leaders regularly ignore ethics, or politics where enough money might change someone's values and votes. Unless you're prepared for these kinds of attacks in this world, your mind and heart will suffer. And you'll likely have a hard time maintaining holiness in your life.

James told us that "real religion" means to "guard against corruption from the godless world" (James 1:27). And Paul said, "Leave the corruption and compromise. . . . Don't link up with those who will pollute you" (2 Corinthians 6:17). But whoa! What do you do when everything around you is godless and tries to pollute you?

The Bible tells us that we shouldn't run, locking ourselves away from the rest of the world. In fact, Jesus says, "Let me tell you why you are here. You're here to be salt-seasoning that brings out the God-flavors of this earth. . . . You're here to be light, bringing out the God-colors in the world" (Matthew 5:13-14). We're never told that it will be easy to live in this evil world. In fact, the Bible repeatedly warns us to expect abuse from the world (see John 15:19; 2 Timothy 3:12; 1 Peter 4:3-4).

But while we're here, in this world full of temptations, we need to remain true to our beliefs. Remember the Christian chameleons we talked about in chapter 2. They try to blend in wherever they go. Maybe you know people who are "good Christians" at church, but they spend the rest of their week ignoring God and his Word. They do and say the Christian thing when they're around Christian friends. But the rest of the time, no one would guess that they're Christians, based on their actions or attitudes. You don't want to be known as a chameleon. You want people to see you as a committed Christian who doesn't just go along with the world around you.

It's been said quite a few times: this won't be easy. You need to develop the kinds of convictions about God and holiness that will enable you to stand up to the pressures that the rest of the world will put on you.

One way to begin to strengthen your faith is to make sure that people around you know you're a Christian. This doesn't mean you have to buy and wear every piece of Jesus paraphernalia ever produced. You don't have to put a fish on your car or wear a WWJD bracelet all the time (unless you like that stuff). But you can find ways to let others know about your faith through your words and your actions. Maybe you pray before a test or before your meal at a restaurant. Or maybe when you're asked to go out with some friends on a night you usually go to church, you tell them. Rather than just saying, "I have to do something tonight," you could say, "I'm going to church tonight. Do you wanna go with?" Whatever comes naturally to you that will let others know you're a Christian—do that.

Even if you identify yourself as a Christian, you'll still probably be faced with things that can be hazardous to your faith. Whether it's the movie with all the sex scenes or your boss who tells you to do things you know are wrong, temptations will always be around, trying to bring you down.

How can you protect yourself from the world around you? You can't escape it, right? Well, a psalmist asked the same question—and found the answer: "How can a young person live a clean life? By carefully reading the map of your Word" (Psalm 119:9).

If you're looking for a good way to protect yourself, here's some advice. It's not new, but it's valuable: start looking in the Bible. It has the power to cleanse your mind and to remind you of the evil around you. It helps you stay in close contact with God, your ultimate Protector.

Of course, we can't just think about protecting ourselves from the world. We also need to be concerned for the world around us. Remember the salt and light passage—Matthew 5:13-14? As salt, we're like a seasoning, something that brings out the best in the world. And we need to be like salt before refrigerators existed—a preservative that delays the world from decaying and dying. As light, we can show others the way to Jesus. We need to be the beacon of light that draws people out of darkness and into the light of Jesus.

It can be tough to be salt and light when we're busy trying to guard our hearts. But if you're really trying to help others find their way to God, he'll give you the strength to resist whatever sins those people may be wrapped up in.

The one thing we can't do while trying to be salt and light is to judge or condemn those around us. If you tell someone, "Hey, I think you're a huge sinner and you need Jesus," his or her natural inclination may be to turn around and judge you right back for your hypocritical attitude. The best thing you can do is to show a genuine love and concern for that person.

Remember, Jesus hung out with drunks and prostitutes. But he didn't preach at them, saying, "You people are so messed up. You're going to spend eternity in hell if you don't change your ways and become like me." Instead, Jesus loved them. He fed and clothed people who were hungry and poor. He ate meals with people no one else in the community would even talk to. As you express your concern for people in the world, learn from Jesus not to condemn them but to love them. Through that love, they'll see Jesus much more clearly than they would through any judgment you might heap on them.

Now, don't misunderstand all of this. Not all Christians are strong enough to withstand being in a situation that could bring them down. If a great temptation for you is drinking too much, it's probably not smart for you to go to parties where you know alcohol will be in abundance. If you really struggle with lust, you should avoid movies or websites that show you a little too much. Sometimes you just need to leave a situation rather than stay and try to be strong. And if you ever end up in a situation that you just can't get out of—pray! Remember that all things are possible with God, even resisting sins that want to control you.

Keep in mind, as you think about all this, that Jesus ate with sinners but didn't become like them. While you're trying to be salt and light, remember that you are chasing after holiness. You don't want to be like the people you're with. You want to be like Jesus.

Here's a good reminder from Paul:

> *No test or temptation that comes your way is beyond the course*
> *of what others have had to face. All you need to remember is that*

God will never let you down; he'll never let you be pushed past your limit; he'll always be there to help you come through it.

So, my very dear friends, when you see people reducing God to something they can use or control, get out of their company as fast as you can. (1 Corinthians 10:13-14)

CHAPTER SIXTEEN

THE JOY OF HOLINESS

God's kingdom isn't a matter of what you put in your stomach,
for goodness' sake. It's what God does with your life as he sets it
right, puts it together, and completes it with joy. —ROMANS 14:17

The joy of winning a race—or even just crossing the finish line—is a feeling that runners experience after months of grueling training. The early morning runs, the special diets, the weight training—all of these can be painful and feel like a chore. But when he has the finish line in sight and the crowd is cheering, the runner experiences the joy of all that hard work paying off.

God wants your life as his child to be joyful, not a chore. Jesus said,

"If you keep my commands, you'll remain intimately at home
in my love. That's what I've done—kept my Father's com-
mands and made myself at home in his love.
"I've told you these things for a purpose: that my joy
might be your joy, and your joy wholly mature."
(John 15:10-11)

Simply put, Jesus says that obedience is linked to joy. When you obey God's commands and chase after holiness, you'll experience joy—no matter what life throws your way.

So let's see how holiness produces joy:

- Fellowship with God. David said, "You will fill me with joy in your presence" (Psalm 16:11, NIV). God equals joy. If you are chasing after holiness, you're growing closer to him and you experience joy in his presence.
- The reward to come. We know that we're destined for a great prize at the end of this chase. That should keep us motivated to keep chasing after holiness and to find joy at the finish line.

Joy isn't just the result of a holy life. Joy can also help to produce a holy life. Nehemiah said, "The joy of GOD is your strength!" (Nehemiah 8:10). If you're living a life of disobedience, you miss out on God's joy and hope. But if you see that Jesus rescued you from sin's control and that God provides you with the ability to obey, you'll find hope. Through that hope in Jesus, you begin to have joy. The strength of this joy helps you conquer the sins that keep attacking you.

If you want to experience this joy, you have to make a choice. You have to choose to acknowledge the fact that you're dead to sin—and then you have to say no to it.

This sounds next to impossible. But remember, God gives us everything we need to complete this chase after holiness. He saved us from sin's control when Jesus died on the cross. He gave us the Holy Spirit to help us. He shows us his will in his Word. He never stops working in us to bring us to completion. He places other believers around us who can encourage and help us in the chase. And finally, God answers our prayers when we ask for strength to say no to temptations.

The choice is yours. Will you obey God's commands? Will you get up when you fall and keep running? Will you decide that holiness is worth the sacrifices you have to make?

Because of his nature, it would be impossible for God to tell you to do something that's impossible. He gives you everything you need to chase after holiness in your everyday life. When you choose to run down that path, you'll experience the abundance of joy that Jesus promised to those who obey.

NOTES

CHAPTER 1

1. *Strong's Exhaustive Concordance of the Bible* (New York: Abingdon, 1890), p. 7 of the "Greek Dictionary of the New Testament."
2. Andrew Bonar, *A Commentary on Leviticus* (1846; reprint, Edinburgh: Banner of Truth Trust, 1972), p. 218.

CHAPTER 2

1. Holiness "is characteristically Godlikeness" (G. B. Stevens, in *Hastings Bible Dictionary*, as quoted by W. E. Vine in *An Expository Dictionary of New Testament Words* [1940; single-volume edition, London: Oliphants, 1957], p. 227). Charles Hodge, writing on the phrase "righteousness unto holiness" in Romans 6:19, said, "The proximate result of obedience to God is inward conformity to the Divine image" (*Commentary on the Epistle to the Romans* [1886; reprint, Grand Rapids, Mich.: Eerdmans, 1955], p. 209). A. W. Pink said, "Holiness . . . consists of that internal change or renovation of our souls whereby our minds, affections and wills are brought into harmony with God" (*The Doctrine of Sanctification* [Swengel, Pa.: Bible Truth Depot, 1955], p. 25).
2. Attributes as applied to God refer to his essential qualities and are inferred from Scriptures describing God. His attribute of holiness is taken from such passages as Exodus 15:11, Leviticus 19:2, Psalm 89:35, Isaiah 57:15, and 1 Peter 1:15-16.
3. Stephen Charnock, *The Existence and Attributes of God* (reprint, Evansville, Ind.: Sovereign Grace Book Club, 1958), p. 449.
4. Charnock, *The Existence and Attributes of God*, p. 448.

CHAPTER 3

1. Walter Marshall (1692), quoted in A. W. Pink, *The Doctrine of Sanctification* (Swengel, Pa.: Bible Truth Depot, 1955), p. 29.

CHAPTER 4

1. John Brown, *Expository Discourses on 1 Peter* (1848; reprint, Edinburgh: Banner of Truth Trust), 2:106.

CHAPTER 5

1. I'm indebted to Dr. D. Martyn Lloyd-Jones for his helpful exposition of the term "died to sin" in chapter 2 of his book *Romans: An Exposition of Chapter 6 — The New Man* (Edinburgh: Banner of Truth Trust, 1972).

2. Jay E. Adams, *Godliness Through Discipline* (reprint, Grand Rapids, Mich.: Baker, 1973).

CHAPTER 6

1. Adapted from the definition of the heart by the Puritan John Owen in his treatise *Indwelling Sin* (1656) as it appears in *Temptation and Sin* (reprint, Evansville, Ind.: Sovereign Grace Book Club, 1958), p. 170.

CHAPTER 7

1. Dr. D. Martyn Lloyd-Jones, *Romans: An Exposition of Chapter 6 — The New Man* (Edinburgh: Banner of Truth Trust, 1972), p. 144.

2. It is also true that the Holy Spirit is the divine Agent who has made us alive to God (see John 6:63). But we are here considering the results of being delivered from the realm of sin into the realm of God, and the indwelling of the Holy Spirit is one of the results.

CHAPTER 9

1. Cited in Clarence H. Faust and Thomas H. Johnson, eds., *Jonathan Edwards: Representative Selections, with Introduction, Bibliography, and Notes*, rev. ed. (New York: Hill & Wang, 1962), p. 38.

AUTHORS

JERRY BRIDGES is a staff member of The Navigators' Collegiate Ministries, in which he is involved in staff training and also serves as a resource person to those ministering on university campuses.

He has been on the staff of The Navigators since 1955. From 1979 through 1994, he served as vice president for Corporate Affairs. In addition to his work in the Collegiate Ministries, he also serves from time to time as a guest lecturer at several seminaries and speaks at numerous conferences and retreats, both in the U.S. and overseas.

Jerry is the author of several books, including the best-selling *The Pursuit of Holiness*, which has sold more than one million copies. Other titles include: *The Practice of Godliness, Trusting God Even When Life Hurts, Transforming Grace, The Discipline of Grace, The Gospel for Real Life, The Crisis of Caring,* and *The Joy of Fearing God.*

Jerry and his wife, Jane, live in Colorado Springs, Colorado. They have two adult children and five grandchildren.

JAY AND JEN HOWVER grew up in the northwest suburbs of Chicago. They met while working at a Christian camp together in Michigan and got married at that camp in 1996. Jay and Jen both work at Youth Specialties and live in southern California.

Experience God's Word.

The Message Remix
Eugene H. Peterson
Hardback
1-57683-434-4
Bonded Alligator Leather
1-57683-450-6

God's Word was meant to be read and understood. It was first written in the language of the people—of fishermen, shopkeepers, and carpenters. *The Message Remix* gets back to that feel. Plus the new verse-numbered paragraphs make it easier to study.

Promises. Promises. Promises.
Eugene H. Peterson
1-57683-466-2

Everybody's making promises these days.
But who's really true to their word?

God is. Take a look at His promises—promises of a real life and a future. See how knowing them can help you trust God even more.

**The Message:
The Gospel of John
in Contemporary Language**
Eugene H. Peterson
1-57683-432-8

Read what John witnessed as he walked alongside Jesus. Then help others find hope and a new way of life—better and more real than they've ever dreamed of experiencing. Share it with everyone you know!

Get the Bible off your shelf and into your heart.

Memorize This: TMS 3.0
1-57683-457-3

Why memorize anything? Laptops, cell phones, PDAs do all the memorizing for you, right? Well, not really. When you need something RIGHT NOW, it needs to be stored in your heart.

That's how God's Word should be—so when something happens, it's right there. After all, how did Jesus handle temptation? He quoted God's Word in its face. A specialized version of NavPress's successful *Topical Memory System*, this book will help you deal with whatever life throws at you—if the words are in your heart, and not just in your machines.

Practice your faith. Every day.

Read, Think, Pray, Live
A guide to reading the Bible in a new way
Tony Jones
1-57683-453-0

If you want to know Jesus and what He's all about, try doing these four things — read, think, pray, live. It's how your faith can grow. *Lectio divina*, or sacred reading, is a time-tested method used by believers to experience God in a personal and real way.

Tailored for students, this book teaches you how to engage your faith. Learning from a method of contemplative study that has worked for hundreds of years, you'll find yourself challenged and encouraged to get to know God in brand-new ways.

1-800-366-7788
www.th1nkbooks.com

No games, no masks—God accepts us as we are.

Posers, Fakers, & Wannabes
Unmasking the Real You
Brennan Manning and Jim Hancock
1-57683-465-4

God isn't fooled by the games we play, the masks we wear. And as much as we try, we'll never fake our way into his affection.

The best part is, the Father already knows and accepts us exactly as we are. He knows how we think and act; He knows our dreams and fears. Brennan and Jim explain how God's total acceptance of us sets us free to be who we really are.

Let's be honest about masturbation.

The Struggle
Dr. Steven Gerali
1-57683-455-7

Jesus wants to free people from whatever weighs them down — even masturbation. But the silence around this issue insinuates that it's a dirty subject — even to talk about. And yet students are talking about it all the time — on TV, in magazines, on college campuses.

Author Steve Gerali opens an honest and thoughtful dialogue on this controversial subject. By doing so, students will gain a biblical understanding on the topic and finally attain freedom from their shame and guilt.

Available Fall 2003